Dual Language
Bilingual Education

BILINGUAL EDUCATION & BILINGUALISM: 123

Dual Language Bilingual Education

Teacher Cases and Perspectives on Large-Scale Implementation

Kathryn I. Henderson and Deborah K. Palmer

MULTILINGUAL MATTERS
Bristol • Blue Ridge Summit

DOI https://doi.org/10.21832/HENDER8090
Library of Congress Cataloging in Publication Data
A catalog record for this book is available from the Library of Congress.
Names: Henderson, Kathryn I.- author. | Palmer, Deborah K.- author.
Title: Dual Language Bilingual Education: Teacher Cases and Perspectives on
    Large-Scale Implementation/Kathryn I. Henderson and Deborah K. Palmer.
Description: Blue Ridge Summit: Multilingual Matters, 2020. | Series: Bilingual Education
    & Bilingualism: 123 | Includes bibliographical references and index. | Summary: "This
    book explores the role of the teacher in dual language bilingual education (DLBE)
    implementation in a time of nationwide program expansion. It provides case studies of
    teachers in the process of implementing and adapting DLBE and highlights the role of
    teachers as language policymakers"— Provided by publisher.
Identifiers: LCCN 2019050150 (print) | LCCN 2019050151 (ebook) | ISBN 9781788928083
    (paperback) | ISBN 9781788928090 (hardback) | ISBN 9781788928106 (pdf) |
    ISBN 9781788928113 (epub) | ISBN 9781788928120 (kindle edition)
Subjects: LCSH: Education, Bilingual—Case studies. | Education, Bilingual—Study and
    teaching. | Second language acquisition—Case studies. | Second language acquisition--
    Study and teaching.
Classification: LCC LC3719 .H46 2020 (print) | LCC LC3719 (ebook) | DDC 370.117—
    dc23 LC record available at https://lccn.loc.gov/2019050150
LC ebook record available at https://lccn.loc.gov/2019050151

British Library Cataloguing in Publication Data
A catalogue entry for this book is available from the British Library.

ISBN-13: 978-1-78892-809-0 (hbk)
ISBN-13: 978-1-78892-808-3 (pbk)

Multilingual Matters
UK: St Nicholas House, 31-34 High Street, Bristol BS1 2AW, UK.
USA: NBN, Blue Ridge Summit, PA, USA.

Website: www.multilingual-matters.com
Twitter: Multi_Ling_Mat
Facebook: https://www.facebook.com/multilingualmatters
Blog: www.channelviewpublications.wordpress.com

The policy of Multilingual Matters/Channel View Publications is to use papers that
are natural, renewable and recyclable products, made from wood grown in sustainable
forests. In the manufacturing process of our books, and to further support our policy,
preference is given to printers that have FSC and PEFC Chain of Custody certification.
The FSC and/or PEFC logos will appear on those books where full certification has been
granted to the printer concerned.

Typeset by Deanta Global Publishing Services, Chennai, India.
Printed and bound in the UK by the CPI Books Group Ltd.
Printed and bound in the US by NBN.

Contents

Acknowledgements

We would like to acknowledge several people without whom this work would not have been possible. Thank you to Olivia Hernandez and David Kauffman whose support was integral in allowing us to engage in this work. Thank you to our colleagues who collaborated with us on this project at different points: Shannon Fitzsimmons-Doolan, Ramón Martínez, Nancy Roser, Suzanne García-Mateus, Dorothy Wall, Christian Zúñiga, Will Slade and Stefan Berthelsen. Thank you to Caitie Dougherty for your help with editing in the final stages of this manuscript. And a huge thanks to Martha Samaniego for the beautiful artwork on the cover of this book! We want to thank the Gómez and Gómez consultants for introducing dual language bilingual education to the educators in this district and many others throughout Texas. We would like to especially thank the teachers and students in our study. Ustedes l@s maestr@s son l@s verdader@s héroes de la educación bilingüe y de la lucha por un sistema educativo mejor. Este trabajo es por y para ustedes.

Sections of some chapters in this volume have been adapted from previous publications:

CHAPTER 1

A portion of this chapter has been previously published and reproduced with permission:

Palmer, D., Zúñiga, C. and Henderson, K.I. (2015) A dual language revolution in the United States? On the bumpy road from compensatory to enrichment education for bilingual children in Texas. In W.E. Wright, S. Boun and O. García (eds) *Handbook of Bilingual and Multilingual Education* (pp. 447-460). Oxford: Wiley-Blackwell.

CHAPTER 4

Portions of this chapter have been previously published and reproduced with permission:

Zúñiga, C.E., Henderson, K.I. and Palmer, D. (2018) Language policy and social justice: How bilingual teachers use policy mandates to their own ends. *Language and Education* 32 (1), 60-76.

Henderson, K.I. and Palmer, D.K. (2015) Teacher and student language practices and ideologies in a third-grade two-way dual language program implementation. *International Multilingual Research Journal* 9 (2), 75-92.

CHAPTER 5

A portion of this chapter has been previously published and reproduced with permission:

Palmer, D., Henderson, K., Wall, D., Zúñiga, C.E. and Berthelsen, S. (2015) Team teaching among mixed messages: Implementing two-way dual language bilingual education at third grade in Texas. *Language Policy* 15 (4), 393-413.

CHAPTER 6

Portions of this chapter have been previously published and reproduced with permission:

Palmer, D., Martínez, R.A., Mateus, S.G. and Henderson, K. (2014) Reframing the debate on language separation: Towards a vision for translanguaging pedagogies in the dual language classroom. *The Modern Language Journal* 98 (3), 757–772.

Henderson, K.I. and Ingram, M. (2018) 'Mister, you're writing in Spanglish': Fostering spaces for meaning making and metalinguistic connections through teacher translanguaging shifts in the bilingual classroom. *Bilingual Research Journal* 41 (3), 253-271.

1 Large-Scale Implementation of Dual Language Bilingual Education: A Key Moment in History

We are witnessing a transformation in bilingual education in the United States: dual language bilingual education (DLBE) programs are increasing in number across the country, even as the once more common transitional bilingual education (TBE) programs are fading away. On the one hand, this is an exciting development with the potential to positively transform the educational experiences of emerging bilingual students or English language learners (ELLs). DLBE programs promote an additive, enrichment-oriented model for the development of student bilingualism and biliteracy, and are associated with high academic achievement for all students participating (Lessow-Hurley, 2013; Lindholm-Leary, 2005; Rolstad *et al.*, 2005; Steele *et al.*, 2017). Research also suggests DLBE can promote positive bilingual and academic identity construction (García-Mateus & Palmer, 2017; Palmer, 2008; Potowski, 2004; Reyes & Vallone, 2007) and cross-cultural competence (Christian, 1994).

On the other hand, with this transformation comes a responsibility to ensure that DLBE programs serve – and continue to serve – the vulnerable, marginalized populations of emergent bilingual students for whom they were first developed. This has proven to be a tremendous challenge (Cervantes-Soon *et al.*, 2017). Rapid increases in the number of DLBE programs mean that educators are contending not only with the usual challenges of diversity – managing differences along the dimensions of race, class, language and culture – but also with the challenges of large-scale, top-down policy implementation that come with the many layers of language policy (LP) including basic miscommunications, varying interpretations, ideological differences, multiple purposes and goals, and contradictions and tensions (Hornberger & Johnson, 2007; Ricento & Hornberger, 1996). Alongside all of this is the challenge of developing antiracist norms within a society that is governed by white supremacy, an ongoing challenge throughout education but particularly salient in DLBE schools in which children have been intentionally integrated along race, class and language lines.

The purpose of this book is to illustrate the critical and complex role that *teachers* play in the implementation of DLBE programs at any scale. This introductory chapter begins with some historical perspective on the way that race and racism in particular have influenced bilingual education in the United States. Next, we provide an overview of the different bilingual education programs currently offered in the United States, who they were designed to serve and with what ideological grounding, and a detailed explanation of the DLBE model implemented by the teachers in this book. We then discuss the current landscape of DLBE in the United States and the urgency of ensuring educational opportunities for emerging bilingual students. We hope this will contextualize the current DLBE expansion and provide a backdrop for the teacher case studies that follow. The chapter concludes with an overview of the structure of the book.

A Brief History of Bilingual Education in the United States

No matter how far back in human history one chooses to go, one will encounter a great deal of linguistic and cultural diversity in the territory now known as the United States. Indigenous communities inhabited the land for many centuries and spoke over 300 languages, some of which survive today (de Jong, 2011). The arrival of Europeans in the 16th and 17th centuries brought disease, conquest, destruction and more languages, including Spanish, German, Dutch and English, with a range of regional varieties (Crawford, 2004; Kloss, 1998). As European conquerors settled in North America throughout the colonial and early American period, they brought people by force from West Africa as slaves, who carried with them many more languages. Throughout the 18th, 19th and early 20th centuries, more waves of immigrants came from several directions – Europe, Asia, Latin America – bringing with them *more* languages and language varieties. These varied tongues evolved, mixed and combined to form unique ways of talking that are entirely our own.

Although linguistic and cultural diversity has always been a reality in the United States, the nation has long been ambivalent in terms of general attitudes toward this diversity. In certain places or instances, more acceptance of diversity and willingness to incorporate difference into the national identity prevailed, thus embracing more 'additive' (Lambert,

1975) or 'pluralist' discourses. In other instances, less tolerance of diversity and more insistence upon embracing a common language as part of national identity reigned, thus asserting more 'subtractive' or 'assimilationist' discourses (de Jong, 2011).

While 'ambivalence' is one way to characterize the nation's pendulum shift in attitudes toward linguistic diversity, it was not a neutral or arbitrary pendulum. Steeped in a history of settler colonialism and chattel slavery, in most cases US society's leanings toward acceptance or rejection of linguistic diversity have fallen along racial lines. In other words, with the possible exceptions of Spanish (which holds a unique place in the hierarchy of languages in the United States – see more on this below and in García [2014]) and German during the two world wars (Blanton, 2005), languages associated with European countries and with whiteness have largely been more accepted and acceptable than languages that originated in Africa, Asia or indigenous America and therefore associated with nonwhiteness. Although some recent shifts in global geopolitical and economic forces have led to intriguing exceptions to these raciolinguistic hierarchies, such as a growing interest in learning Mandarin among middle- and upper-class Americans, this racially affiliated hierarchy of status for languages remains powerful and salient in US language ideologies (Rosa & Flores, 2017). Languages associated with whiteness such as French and German are still viewed as more worthy of study than languages associated with and used by far larger populations of majority people of color (even populations that live in the United States in large numbers) such as Hindi, Urdu or Malay.

As mentioned, Spanish – after English which is the most widely spoken language in the United States – holds a unique place in American history and society. Spanish is most certainly a European language; it was, in fact, the first colonial language to take root in the territory now known as the United States, and much of the US West, South and southwest still bear evidence of the influence of Spain's 15th- and 16th-century conquest through their place names and in the lively local varieties of the language still spoken (Escobar & Potowski, 2015; Toribio & Bullock, 2016). A large chunk of US territory was still part of Mexico (and Spanish dominant) until the Treaty of Guadalupe Hidalgo in 1847. In that sense, Spanish is a language associated with whiteness, with global influence and with power. Yet, the language is largely glossed in the United States as a marginalized language of immigrants and people of color (i.e. Latinas/os). The case of Spanish in the United States provides a vivid example of the complexities of the ongoing process of joint production of racial and linguistic hierarchies (García, 2014; Rosa & Flores, 2017).

What of schooling then?

Around the early 19th century, when communities began in larger numbers to bring their children together in schools (Tyack & Cuban, 1995), instruction was often in their own languages, sometimes in combination with English, for example German and Dutch in Pennsylvania, French in Louisiana (Kloss, 1998) and Spanish and German in Texas (Blanton, 2005). Notably, these were all European languages. From the beginning, indigenous and African languages have been banned from the official spaces of schooling in the United States (de Jong, 2011).

By the end of the 19th century, when free and compulsory schooling was becoming commonplace, English dominated public schools and education, and other languages became more controversial (Blanton, 2005; Kloss, 1998; Ricento, 2005). This controversy was no doubt triggered by the Industrial Revolution and the 'great wave' of immigration that began in the 1880s, bringing new immigrants from Eastern and Southern Europe who spoke new languages such as Greek, Italian and Polish. Many established white Americans, having arrived in previous generations from countries in Western Europe, drew a line between themselves and these new immigrants. The privilege of whiteness would be denied the new immigrants for several generations (Roediger, 2005). It was during this period of xenophobia that widespread public schooling embraced the primary purpose of 'Americanizing' or assimilating new immigrants from Southern and Eastern Europe into an English-speaking Anglo-Saxon America (Schmid, 2000; Tyack & Cuban, 1995). Two world wars and an era of political and economic isolationism in the first half of the 20th century merely exacerbated this shift in the national discourse toward more extreme assimilationism. Blanton (2005) documents this period in Texas history, when English-only education became a rigid statewide policy in schools despite obvious evidence that it was failing massive numbers of Mexican-American children. Speaking and using exclusively English (and striving to achieve whiteness) had become inextricably associated with an American identity (Orellana *et al.*, 1999; Ricento, 2005).

Meanwhile, indigenous languages, having been discouraged from the beginning, became a direct target of the government during this period. English-only policies dominated – and still dominate – schools for native children. From the 1860s to the 1970s, in an explicit government effort to eradicate their languages and cultures, native children across the United States were forcibly removed from their families and sent to English-only boarding schools in which they were subjected to harsh punishments if they used their own languages (Santa Ana, 2004).

Bilingual education in the modern era: The resurgence of bilingual education as a compensatory program

In the 1960s, federal education policy in the United States experienced a return to bilingual education, but the story illustrates the continued tension between assimilationist and pluralist discourses, and a continued racial hierarchy for languages. The 1968 Bilingual Education Act (BEA) – Title VII of the Federal Elementary and Secondary Education Act – allowed districts and schools to apply for grants to try 'experimental programs' in languages other than English in schools, thus opening up a pluralist space. Yet, after long debate and much compromise in Congress, ultimately the language of the BEA made these programs compensatory, justifying their expense by the special 'needs' of bilingual students, a majority of whom in that era were Spanish-speaking students of color, from Puerto Rico in the northeast or Mexico in the southwest (Blanton, 2005; Crawford, 2004). In other words, the language within national bilingual education policy during this time signaled a need to remedy or fix a problem – linguistic diversity as a problem – positioning emerging bilinguals in a negative way, rather than promoting linguistic rights and the value of bilingualism – linguistic diversity as a right and resource – positioning emerging bilinguals in an additive way (Ruiz, 1984). In 1974, the *Lau v. Nichols* Supreme Court decision ruled that educators had a responsibility to provide 'affirmative remedial efforts to give special attention to linguistically deprived children'. Largely, the term 'linguistically deprived' was applied to children who spoke a range of Asian or indigenous languages, or Spanish. School districts suddenly found themselves needing to bridge home and school languages in order to comply with the required accommodations for 'limited English proficient' (LEP) students. TBE programs were conceived as one possible solution to compensate for emergent bilingual children's lack of English fluency in the early years of schooling. Such compensatory or remedial programs brought some mother tongue education back into schools, but at the cost of viewing children's own linguistic and cultural resources as a handicap (Ricento, 2005).

Politics of English-only vs English-plus: Contention in language policy debates

Starting in the 1980s, movements against bilingual education resurfaced, hampering the programmatic progress in bilingual education during the previous two decades. Driven by nationalist, xenophobic forces, anti-bilingual groups formed, including US English, English-only and English First, representing a monolingual and assimilationist ideology whose rhetoric displayed thinly veiled efforts to protect whiteness (Citrin *et al.*, 1990; Wiley & Lukes, 1996). Indeed, the Reagan administration represented this ideology; President Reagan himself stated, 'It is absolutely wrong and against American concepts to have a bilingual education program that is now openly, admittedly dedicated to preserving their native language and never getting them adequate in English so they can go out into the job market and participate' (National Archives and Records Administration, 1981). Despite the increase in public anti-bilingual education sentiment, there remained an important advocacy presence (Ovando, 2003). In 1975, the National Association of Bilingual Education (NABE) formed, which remains active to the present, and in 1985 an organization called English Plus launched. Nonetheless, during this period these pro-bilingual organizations garnered less public support than their anti-bilingual counterparts.

This growing English-only movement gained ground in the 1990s and early 2000s, shifting federal policy back to assimilationist orientations. The BEA ended in 2002. Voter initiatives, funded by Silicon Valley businessman Ron Unz, rationalized as efforts to end segregated bilingual programs and instead offer 'better' educational opportunity to linguistically marginalized children of color resulted in laws restricting the language of instruction in elementary schools to English in California (1998), Arizona (2000) and Massachusetts (2002).

At the time of writing, those initiatives in Massachusetts and California have essentially been overturned. However, in the process of winning these fights with public opinion, advocates have shifted the rationale for bilingual programs: instead of framing bilingual education as a compensatory program to support children who are learning English in school, bilingual education – going under the name of 'dual language' education – is now for the purpose of giving *all* children opportunities to become bilingual and biliterate in school. Thus, bilingual education advocates appear to have intentionally sidestepped compensatory arguments, and along with this have managed to sidestep the oblique raciolinguistic ideologies that have plagued bilingual education politics for several generations (Cervantes-Soon, 2018; Flores, 2016). In other words, the racialized and linguistically subtractive history of bilingual education is hidden. This is symbolized through the disappearance of the term 'bilingual' within 'dual language'. The use of the term 'dual language bilingual education' or DLBE rather than 'dual language' is an intentional choice to recognize this history (see Sánchez *et al.*, 2017).

This strategy appears to be having widespread success. Over the past 20 years, even as TBE programs have become less popular, the numbers of enrichment-oriented 'dual language' bilingual education (DLBE) programs have continued to increase (Center for Applied Linguistics, 2016; Wilson, 2011). School districts and state departments of education are embracing DLBE programs for large-scale implementation, and some recent estimates show that there are over 3000 such programs in the United States – and growing (Fausset, 2019). This growth continues despite increasingly blatant nationalist and xenophobic discourse emerging across the United States and the increasing numbers of hate crimes connected to these discourses (Beirich, 2019).

Meanwhile, regardless of the tone and tenor of public debate and even despite increasingly harsh immigration policies designed to deter particularly non-white immigrants from crossing the country's southern border, linguistic diversity also continues to increase across the United States. The number of people in the United States who speak a language other than English at home has more than doubled since 1990 and almost tripled since 1980 (US Department of Education, 2015). Currently, it is estimated that nearly one in four students in school in the United States comes from a home where another language is spoken (US Department of Education, 2015). In Texas, the context for this book, the estimate is one in three. Emerging bilingual students have been underserved by the educational system (Valdés, 2001; Valenzuela, 1999). The historical and ongoing systemic disservice to this student population is a significant social and economic issue for the United States and DLBE represents a potential opportunity for positive change. Critical examination of the complexities involved in large-scale, top-down DLBE implementation from the teacher perspective can contribute in this direction.

Bilingual Education Program Models and the 'Dual Language Revolution'

Depending on state and local policies, schools have a range of program choices for serving emergent bilingual children. Programs labeling themselves as *English as a second language* (ESL) or *structured English immersion* (SEI) focus on teaching children English and generally spend little or no energy supporting the development of children's home languages, thus reinforcing the primacy of English as a signifier of American identity and power. *Bilingual* programs meanwhile make use of children's first language in school or provide instruction in two languages (English and a partner language). Some programs are more *transitional* in nature, using children's first language or the partner language for only a short time and expecting them to shift within a few years to all-English instruction. In their design and overarching goals – to transition children to English-only education as quickly as possible – these TBE programs emerge from a compensatory ideology around emerging bilingual students, though many TBE teachers are deeply invested in supporting their students' bilingualism and biliteracy over the long term (Palmer, 2011).

Other programs are more *developmental*, emphasizing children's development of high levels of biliteracy. Recently, these latter enrichment program models have also taken on the label *dual language bilingual education* (DLBE). The Center for Applied Linguistics (CAL) (2016) defines dual language education as programs in which, 'students are taught literacy and academic content in English and a partner language. The goals of DLBE are for students to develop high levels of language proficiency and literacy in both program languages, to demonstrate high levels of academic achievement, and to develop an appreciation for and an understanding of diverse cultures'. In other words, DLBE programs share three core goals for their students: (a) bilingualism/biliteracy; (b) grade-level (or above) academic achievement; and (c) cross-cultural competencies (or biculturalism). Recently, some researchers including Deb (Author 2) (Cervantes-Soon *et al.*, 2017; Freire, 2016) have proposed adding a fourth core goal – (d) critical or sociopolitical consciousness – to the definition of DLBE programs, in an effort to ensure that all stakeholders in these educational programs are aware of – and actively working to counter – disparities between students with different race, class or language backgrounds.

DLBE programs also generally share a set of characteristics including content taught through language and language through content; standard grade-level curriculum; frequent use of pair/group work and sheltered instruction throughout the school day; program duration of at least six consecutive years; and an intentional structured use of the two (or more) 'program languages' (Howard *et al.*, 2018). DLBE programs can serve different student populations. The terminology can be confusing, so let's take a moment to clarify the way we are understanding the program labels. The term '*one-way* DLBE' has been used in two ways: in much of the United States, this term refers to 'foreign' language immersion programs – i.e. programs designed to immerse dominant English-speaking students in a new language. However, in most of Texas (including the district where this project took place), '*one-way* DLBE' refers to programs that serve a community of emerging bilingual students, all of whom share a home language. These programs have historically been called 'developmental bilingual education' programs; however, to match the terminology of the district we partnered with, we will call them 'one-way DLBE' programs.

Two-way DLBE programs, meanwhile (confusingly sometimes referred to as 'dual immersion' or 'two-way bilingual' or even just generally as 'dual language' programs), are designed to serve a relatively 'balanced' population of initially English-dominant students and students who are initially dominant in the 'target' non-English language of the program. Elsewhere, we have taken issue with this rather stringent definition for the population of two-way programs, and pushed back against what we've argued is an arbitrary line drawn between these program types (Henderson & Palmer, 2015a, 2019). We have pointed out that the bilingualism/biliteracy reality in classrooms full of real children is far messier than this 50/50 population mandate would imply, especially as more and more children in the United States begin their lives someplace along a bilingual continuum (Escamilla *et al.*, 2014). Students linguistic repertoires reflect the complex sociolinguistic characteristics of their multilingual communities, and engineering which types of students should enroll in different programs doesn't reflect this reality (García, Menken, Velasco & Vogel, 2018). Indeed, it will become clear in the cases we describe in this book that the one-way/two-way dichotomy needs refining. However, for the purposes of clarity, we will continue to use these labels as they were used in the school district and by the teachers.

Many one-way and two-way DLBE programs in the United States began as local grassroots initiatives, supported by government or private grants, involving local deliberation and decision-making. The very first two-way DLBE program, at Coral Way Elementary in Florida, began in 1963 to accommodate Cuban refugees, determined that their children should maintain high academic levels of Spanish. The school also included the Cuban children's English-speaking neighbors, in approximately equal numbers (Crawford, 2004). A hybrid of the French immersion program for majority (English) language-speaking children in Canada and the developmental bilingual education program for minority language-speaking children in the United States, the new 'two-way immersion' program was a success. Other schools in intensely linguistically diverse urban centers followed in its tracks, such as the Amigos program in Cambridge, Massachusetts (Cazabon *et al.*, 1997); the Oyster Bilingual program in Washington, DC (Freeman, 1998); the River Glen program in San Jose, California; and the Interamerican Magnet School in Chicago, Illinois (Christian *et al.*, 1997). Over many years, the number of DLBE programs in the United States grew gradually, offering specialized opportunities to a small number of children with perhaps one or two schools in a region choosing to take on the challenge.

Research identifies certain advantages to bottom-up (grassroots) initiatives (Darling-Hammond, 1990) including in the implementation of DLBE programs specifically (Freeman, 2004; Pérez, 2004). Bottom-up implementation processes tend to foster unity around the purpose, and better ensure that all parties involved are well informed, prepared and invested in the process. Pérez (2004) described the process of bottom-up planning and implementation of two-way dual language strands in two elementary schools in San Antonio, Texas. She found that the leadership and commitment to parent participation allowed for continual negotiation of the implementation process, ultimately resulting in strong advocacy for the program across groups of people. The whole community coming together, including administrators, parents, teachers, researchers and students, was critical for the process of dual language implementation and maintenance of the program (Pérez, 2004). Similarly, Freeman (2004) described her involvement as a consultant for the implementation of DLBE in Philadelphia at several self-selected elementary schools, in which the school staff and parent leadership teams engaged in a full year of learning and planning before beginning implementation of their own unique, context-specific models for DLBE.

In the past 15 years, however, a sort of 'dual language revolution' has been occurring as an estimated 2000–3000 DLBE programs have sprouted up nationwide (Center for Applied Linguistics, 2016; Fausset, 2019; Wilson, 2011). The increasing number of programs can be attributed, in part, to the unprecedented expansion of large-scale implementation initiatives, in which entire states and/or entire school districts are implementing DLBE. The strength of commitment born from grassroots initiatives is unlikely to be present in a school experiencing top-down imposition of a DLBE program. And yet, top-down, large-scale implementation does open a space for substantially more students to participate in an enrichment bilingual model – and sooner. School leaders across a range of states from Alaska to North Carolina have committed to district-wide DLBE implementation (Center for Applied Linguistics, 2016). Currently, 17 states have an explicit state-level DLBE policy (Freire & Delavan, under review). Utah introduced a state-level DLBE policy in 2008, and the Utah model has been followed by five additional states: Georgia, Delaware, Wyoming, Rhode Island and Indiana (Freire & Delavan, under review; Utah Dual Language immersion, 2018). Texas, where well over 80 school districts (representing more than 600 schools) have adopted district-wide

DLBE, appears to be a driving force in the movement (Center for Applied Linguistics, 2016).

The widespread district-level implementation in Texas has largely been made possible by a specific program model emerging from Texas' Rio Grande Valley, developed by Dr Richard Gómez and Dr Leo Gómez (Dual Language Training Institute, 2018; Gómez *et al.*, 2005) The Gómez and Gómez Dual Language Enrichment model seems to have hit upon a winning message that attracts policymakers and district administrators to an 'additive' and 'enrichment' model of bilingual education in the interests of improving academic outcomes (e.g. increasing test scores) for bilingual students. This was the model implemented in the school district that we studied, and so it warrants closer attention.

Understanding the Gómez and Gómez program

The Gómez and Gómez model from South Texas incorporates many of the key elements that the DLBE research literature recommends for high-quality DLBE programs. The model deliberately pairs students for cooperative group work across 'language groups' (i.e. pairing an 'English-dominant' student with a 'Spanish-dominant' student), building in opportunities for communicative practice. In 'two-way' Gómez-Gómez contexts, there is the expectation of team teaching (Gómez *et al.*, 2005; Howard, Sugarman & Christian, 2003). The model also clearly mandates the deliberate separation of languages by content area for instruction in academic registers of Spanish and English, along with alternating a 'language of the day' for incidentals and transitions. To be sure, the dictated LP in the Gómez and Gómez program is complicated; even if following it strictly, a teacher could find himself/herself switching from English to Spanish and back again several times within the span of a morning. In the Gómez-Gómez 50/50 content model, math is always taught in English, while social studies and science are always expected to be taught in Spanish. For language arts, children receive initial literacy instruction – for their first three years in school – in their 'primary' or 'dominant' language and are thus separated by language group for this chunk of every day. After three years (which is usually second or third grade), all students are expected to receive a balanced one hour of language arts instruction in each of the program languages.

Importantly, due to the segregation of students for language arts during children's first three years in the program, initially English-dominant students do not receive 50% of their instruction in the 'partner' (non-dominant) language within the Gómez and Gómez two-way DLBE program, which does not align with the guiding principles of dual language (Howard *et al.*, 2018: 15). Children who are designated as English dominant in pre-kindergarten or kindergarten (whenever they begin school) will only receive their social studies and science instruction in Spanish during their first three years, along with occasional 'language of the day' lessons and instructions in Spanish.

Another important complicating factor related to the segregation of students for language arts has to do with identifying students' 'dominant' or 'primary' language. For some students, this is a straightforward process; but for many, especially in South Texas, students' primary language really is *both* Spanish and English. The decision of which language to assign to children can be a challenging one for educators, and a harrowing one for parents, all of which seems a bit counterproductive if the purpose of the program is to encourage all students to be – and become – bilingual, biliterate and bicultural (Henderson & Palmer, 2019; Palmer, 2019).

This speaks to the broader controversial issue of strict language separation in DLBE or the practice of strictly separating program languages for use with different content areas or on different days/weeks/times of day, justified by the argument that without such rigidity, i.e. protected times during the day to practice each program language, children would not be motivated to engage in their non-dominant language and would never master the standard register. We, along with others, have argued that such strict separation is artificial, that since bilinguals have the ability to draw on language features across their repertoire, more linguistic flexibility – thoughtful linguistically responsive pedagogy – should be encouraged in order to best develop bilingualism and support rich academic learning and deep thinking (García, 2009a; García & Kleyn, 2016; Palmer, Martínez, Mateus & Henderson, 2014). The field is currently proposing and exploring new DLBE models that incorporate times for bilingual language practice, in which languages are intentionally integrated and students are encouraged to develop cross-linguistic and metalinguistic skills and to engage in deeply explaining their thinking without attention to which code they use (e.g. Sánchez *et al.*, 2017). However, like the Gómez and Gómez model, the vast majority of programs still maintain a strict separation of program languages, encouraging children to engage monolingually in each program language. The tension between implementing a model with strict language separation and serving students whose 'first language' (L1) might best be described as Spanglish (or Spanish of the Southwest or TexMex) is a theme that will be given attention at different points in the book.

The Gómez and Gómez 'Elementary Dual Language Enrichment' model is copyrighted under the Dual Language Training Institute (2018) which holds exclusive rights for training and authorizing its use. Teams from the institute provide one-day training for district and school administrators and three-day training for all classroom teachers prior to implementation, with follow-up classroom visits for all participating classrooms midway through the school year for the initial years of implementation. The Gómez and Gómez model recommends that implementation begins with the youngest students only, with each successive grade level taking on the program model as participating children reach it, thus fully implementing the program within approximately five years. District administrators have only to sign the contract with the Gómez and Gómez consulting team in order to begin the transformational DLBE process.

On the surface, this transformation indeed seems revolutionary. However, the devil is in the details; the primarily top-down implementation appears to have mixed results when confronted with the realities of different school contexts and different educator language ideologies. This large-scale attempt to shift program orientation throughout a large and populous state provides a forum for a dramatic surfacing of the often-contradictory discourses around language and education that prevail in Texas and throughout the United States. Furthermore, despite the promise of DLBE, the reality – even when programs are implemented on a small scale at local level – is far more complicated. We will turn now to the question of equity in DLBE.

Equity and the Current Landscape of DLBE

The current state of bilingual education in the United States reflects its contentious history and remains complicated and contradictory. On the one hand, anti-bilingual education sentiment and assimilationist policies and language ideologies persist. Educational policy replacing BEA, including No Child Left Behind (NCLB) and its successor the Every Student Succeeds Act (ESSA), along with the recent Common Core State Standards adopted by over half of the states, continues to reflect an assimilationist ideology and prioritize English-only (Evans & Hornberger, 2005; Valdés *et al.*, 2015), barely making mention of the growing population of bilingual students in US schools and pressuring schools to show increasing improvement on English-only standardized tests (Menken, 2009). This has the effect of actually decreasing the number of bilingual education programs, even in places such as New York City where such programs are mandated (Menken & Solorza, 2014). Furthermore, the negative rhetoric spread by organizations and people who denounce bilingualism has arguably intensified assimilationist ideologies – or emboldened individuals who articulate and embody them – under the current anti-immigrant administration.

At the same time, the overwhelming majority of empirical studies continue to report on the advantages of bilingualism and bilingual education (Adesope *et al.*, 2010; Callahan & Gándara, 2014; Rolstad *et al.*, 2005; Umansky & Reardon, 2014). Building on this research, new pluralist language ideologies praising the benefits of bilingualism and bilingual education surfaced within the media, describing bilingualism's potential cognitive benefits, including improved executive function and later onset of dementia (Craik *et al.*, 2010; Martin-Rhee & Bialystok, 2008; McQuillan & Tse, 1996). California (2016), followed by Massachusetts (2018), reversed English-only policy, opening space for significant bilingual education development. And, of course, the number of DLBE programs increased substantially (Center for Applied Linguistics, 2016). In sum, the current ideological landscape appears highly polarized.

Yet, in terms of understanding the impacts of linguistic ideologies on the schooling experiences of linguistically diverse students at the local level, it is insufficient to describe the language ideological landscape in the United States as polarizing. Regardless of larger historical trends, during every time period, conflicting language ideologies have *always* co-existed (Ovando, 2003). Schools in particular remain a primary site of 'language ideological combat' (Alim, 2007: 163). More recent conceptualizations of language ideology recognize the multiple and even contradictory nature of language ideologies (Gal, 1998; Henderson, 2019; Kroskrity, 1998; Woolard, 1998). Multiple, competing ideologies exist within the state (Freeman, 2004), school (Alim, 2007), district (Hornberger & Johnson, 2007) and even the individual educator (Henderson & Palmer, 2015a, 2015b; Martínez, 2013; Martínez *et al.*, 2014; Palmer, 2011) and bilingual child (Dorner, 2010). A meaningful exploration into bilingual education must consider more complex ideological relationships.

Indeed, understanding the current climate of DLBE requires critical examination of *why* these programs are increasing in number and popularity, and *for whom*. Although DLBE programs are often touted as the very best model for emerging bilingual students, equity of access and opportunity within DLBE programs is not straightforward. Addressing the two-way DLBE program specifically, Valdés (1997) sent a 'cautionary note' to bilingual educators and researchers addressing the potential biasing of programs in favor of Anglo students rather than their language-minoritized peers. She expressed several concerns: that instruction in non-dominant languages would be 'watered down' to accommodate English-dominant learners; that while learning a new language was an enrichment for English-speaking children, learning English was an absolute necessity (and was absolutely expected) for children who came to school dominant in other languages; and that the imbalance of power between English and the minority language will matter in the classroom (Valdés, 1997).

Since Valdés' influential piece, multiple researchers have explored these potential asymmetries (see Cervantes-Soon *et al.* [2017] for a review of this research). Unfortunately, she turned out to have been quite prescient; inequities have been uncovered at multiple levels in DLBE, and the effort to create equitable spaces for learning is extremely complex (in DLBE as in any schooling context). In some places, DLBE program expansion explicitly focuses on serving English-dominant-speaking children (Valdez *et al.*, 2016). The overturning of English-only legislation has been interwoven with a rebranding of bilingual education through neoliberal and global human capital discourse (Katznelson & Bernstein, 2017) that explicitly advertises the learning of multiple languages as a valuable skill for 21st-century global citizens, with little regard for the communities and cultures that occupy those languages. Some research has documented school systems granting or limiting access to DLBE programs to people from different communities or language backgrounds, implying that not all are welcomed and valued in these elite spaces (Dorner, 2011; Scanlan & Palmer, 2009). Schoolwide language and assessment policies have been documented to undermine the goals of their own DLBE programs (Henderson & Palmer, 2015a, 2015b; Palmer, 2007) or to treat different communities within their programs differently (Pimentel *et al.*, 2008). Educators at different levels of implementation adopt exclusionary and elitist discourse that promotes a vision of DLBE for only select students (Henderson, 2019). Within classrooms, interaction patterns have been shown to favor English-dominant, middle-class students (Chaparro, 2019a; Palmer, 2009) and curricula have been observed to center dominant narratives, thus marginalizing the histories and positions of the children whose language and culture they were designed to center (Heiman & Yanes, 2018). Even in contexts where parents, administrators and teachers have clearly adopted the stated goals of a DLBE program, students have been observed to take on ideologies of English dominance themselves despite the concerted efforts of adults (Chaparro, 2019a; Dorner, 2010). Larger structures of power, beyond the schoolhouse doors, also influence DLBE programs; communities in transition lead to schools in transition. Gentrification, for example, has been documented to have a negative impact on DLBE school communities (Chaparro, 2019b; Heiman, 2017). Thus, it is clear that while the additive ideological underpinnings of DLBE are promising – and necessary – if we want to support equitable learning opportunities for bilingual and emergent bilingual youth, there are many pitfalls. We most definitely need more research to better understand these complicated spaces in order to leverage them for equity.

One place to start is by challenging the static ideological designation for particular program types and models. Labels are always more complicated than they may at first seem. While one might attempt to assign the blanket labels of *assimilationist* to ESL/SEI programs and *pluralist* to dual language programs and policy (de Jong, 2011), a great deal depends on the beliefs and practices of the individual teachers and school leaders who design and carry out school programs (Menken & García, 2010). There are ESL teachers, for example, who despite their own lack of knowledge of the languages spoken by their students, make tremendous effort to reach out to linguistically diverse families and to offer children access to materials in their mother tongue. At the same time, there are teachers in programs that bear the label *dual language* whose main goal appears to be to encourage children to leave their home languages behind and learn to function entirely in English in school. Program labels, in other words, often tell us little about what discourses abound in schools and classrooms (Menken & García, 2010; Palmer, 2011). These discourses are constantly shifting, and the only way to understand them is to venture inside classrooms to speak with educators.

This is precisely what this book attempts to do: to take readers inside the classrooms of six very different educators, working in different schools, reacting to the challenges of implementing a DLBE program that was mandated in over 65 schools across a large, diverse, urban school district in Texas. Thus far, the field has not adequately addressed DLBE policy and implementation from the teacher perspective. Given the rapid expansion of DLBE programs, we saw an urgent need for an educator resource detailing teachers' perception of the successes and challenges of DLBE implementation, particularly in new, large-scale, top-down implementation contexts.

The specific teacher case studies in this book offer windows into classroom-level teacher decision-making, language practices and policy implementation. All the teachers were working within the same district, under the same set of policy mandates, having undergone the same DLBE teacher professional development. Yet, as you will see, the cases diverge starkly. We will draw attention to the tensions and contradictions that emerge when an LP is imposed upon teachers with different backgrounds, experiences and ideologies in unique local contexts. Tensions and contradictions exist not only across teacher cases, but also within each classroom, necessitating dynamic analytic frameworks that are non-static and non-binary. Ultimately, we hope you will see that LP implementation is an ongoing, iterative, multifaceted process in which teachers play a critical and complex role.

Structure of the Book

Chapter 2 introduces the LP framework and the language ecology perspective that we draw on to analyze and contextualize teachers' classroom LP implementation processes. In Chapter 3, we provide an overview of the larger study from which these cases emerged, with a detailed description of the many layers of data collection and analysis that took place. We talk about the context for the study, offering some description of the district and city. We then provide an overarching analysis of educator experiences with the implementation of DLBE in the district as a whole, drawing on district-wide survey and interview data.

Chapters 4–6 comprise the heart of the book – the teacher case studies. They offer glimpses into classrooms and teachers' professional efforts to provide excellent learning opportunities for their bilingual students within sometimes very challenging policy contexts. Each chapter presents *two* teacher cases, and focuses primarily on *one* of the key tensions/issues that emerged in the analysis. Chapter 4 focuses on two teachers, Marisol and Rachel, who aimed to implement the program with fidelity and the tension with classroom language policy and practices that did not fit the model. Chapter 5 exposes the struggle of two teachers, Mariana and Lisel, to implement an additive bilingual program alongside the pressure for student achievement on monolingual standardized assessment. Chapter 6 presents two teachers, Olivia and Michael, who adapted the model to the local context with a focus on the issue of balancing modifications with programmatic requirements. The thematic structure broadly represents the spectrum of implementation outcomes: (a) implementation with fidelity to the model (Chapter 4); (b) failure to implement the model (Chapter 5); and (c) implementation of the model with local adaptation (Chapter 6). That said, it is in the nature of qualitative case study research that these multiple instrumental cases merged and overlapped, sometimes echoing and sometimes contradicting one another. Our hope is that this will help us convey the complexity of policy implementation at the classroom level.

Finally, Chapter 7 brings together our reflections on the set of cases and offers recommendations. Our goal was to attempt to provide guidance to teachers and school leaders (and those who prepare them) faced with similar policy impositions, in order that they might make the most of the opportunity to create the kinds of equitable, engaging, diverse learning spaces that DLBE promises.

2 Guiding Theories: A Language Policy and Language Ecology Framework for Exploring DLBE Program Implementation

The implementation of a dual language bilingual education (DLBE) program, like any comprehensive language-in-education policy, is inherently challenging. Actors at every level of the implementation process contribute their own interpretations, with sometimes incomplete or contradictory results. In a US context, given the predominance of monolingual ideologies or the belief that everyone should speak one language – in this context English – in schools and society, challenges abound. In this chapter, we begin by presenting the theoretical and methodological frameworks guiding our research: we explored teachers as language policymakers grounded in a language policy (LP) and planning framework, carrying out a four-year ethnography of policy implementation (Hornberger & Johnson, 2007, 2011; Menken & García, 2010). This approach, grounded in a language ecology perspective and combined with social theory for analyzing classroom interactions, allowed us to pick apart and understand the specific kinds of work that teachers did, constructing identities and policies in their classrooms as they engaged in the implementation of a DLBE policy in this large urban school district. We also aimed to both uncover educator language ideologies – teacher beliefs about language – and use them as a tool for analysis of classroom interaction and local LP. As such, we will discuss how we view language, define language ideology, and provide a review of the literature on DLBE program implementation particularly as it relates to teachers working in the United States.

Language Policy

We draw on an LP framework to explore DLBE implementation from the teacher perspective. More specifically, our approach to this investigation draws on the metaphor of an onion to investigate different 'layers' of LP (Hornberger & Johnson, 2007, 2011; Ricento & Hornberger, 1996). The different layers of the metaphorical LP onion include (from outer to inner): national legislation, states and agencies, institutions (i.e. districts and book publishers) and local practitioners. Each layer permeates and is permeated by the others; when LP is passed, enacted or, in this case, mandated at one of these levels, it is reinterpreted and renegotiated by the local actors at each of the other levels (Hornberger & Johnson, 2011; Ricento & Hornberger, 1996). The implementation of national LP at the state level will look different based on the local state actors involved (Hornberger & Johnson, 2011; Ricento & Hornberger, 1996). For example, in the state of Texas, education policy mandates that 'Each school district that has an enrollment of 20 or more English learners in any language classification in the same grade level district-wide shall offer a bilingual education program (TEC §89.1205)'. For many years, the school district where we carried out this study interpreted this mandate narrowly, offering early-exit transitional bilingual education in kindergarten, first and sometimes second grades. Even though certain classrooms were designated as 'bilingual' in the upper elementary grades, very little Spanish was used in most schools, especially past second or third grade. Even during this period, however, individual teachers would embrace an enriching bilingual perspective, supporting their students' development of higher levels of biliteracy despite district policy, much like the educators portrayed in Chapter 6. Thus, state policy influences local district policy, which in turn has influence upon classroom policies – each layer of this onion has agency, and local interpretations matter.

This LP perspective, which takes into account stakeholders across different levels, affords researchers the tools for a multilayered LP analysis. With these tools, we can make connections between different layers of LP, exploring for example the ways that national LP and state LP interact and influence one another (Gándara & Baca, 2008) or the connections between state, local and classroom language policies (Hornberger & Johnson, 2007; Johnson, 2010; Marschall *et al.*, 2011). Our focus in this book is on the metaphorical heart of the onion: the teachers. We sought to understand how teachers interpreted and enacted the district's DLBE LP and considered how different layers of policy implementation impacted the construction of their classroom language policies including the kinds of language practices that took place.

An additional advantage of this framework is the ability to identify and locate tensions between the distinct LP layers. Macro and micro LP tension is perpetuated by the highly interpretive nature of much LP (Wright, 2004). Interpretability opens up space for local actors at all levels of LP to defend or fight for their social, political and/or economic interests (Hornberger & Johnson, 2011; Phillips, 2003; Ricento & Hornberger, 1996). For example, Phillips (2003) argued that LP in the United States in relation to foreign language programs has been haphazard, vague and/or indirect. As such, the degree and extent to which LP affected the instruction of foreign languages in schools and universities has often been by chance or mediated through local actors. Another example is the tremendous variation state-by-state and school-by-school in what was labeled 'bilingual education' after the passing of the Bilingual Education Act in 1968 (Hornberger & Johnson, 2011; Ricento & Hornberger, 1996). The ideologies embedded in the policies interacted with the individual ideologies of the local state and school actors to produce tension that manifested in radically different policy implementation (Hornberger & Johnson, 2011; Ricento & Hornberger, 1996). Chapters 4–6 in this book will demonstrate tensions within LP layers that occurred between the district DLBE LP and the interpretation, negotiation and enactment of that policy by DLBE teachers in their classrooms. These tensions arose in different ways based on the LP demands placed on the teachers at different schools, and the individual and professional language and language teaching experiences of the teachers.

Thus, the agency of local actors – in this case, the agency of the DLBE teachers – becomes of critical importance. Research on teacher agency in bilingual education for local instructional decisions within a larger conflicting macro LP has mixed findings. On the one hand, research has found that teachers' agency can be limited based on LP demands. For example, Palmer (2011) explored transitional bilingual educators and identified the tension between the teachers' ideological positioning toward additive bilingualism and their program requirement to transition students to English. Despite their beliefs, teachers were pressured to transition and, ultimately, adopted the transition process as the ultimate goal. It appears that transitional Spanish/English bilingual programs can be a space where teacher and students' ideologies of English dominance overrun spaces for Spanish interaction.

On the other hand, additional research has shown how teachers have agency to engage in instructional practices that align with their beliefs. Olson (2009) explored English language learner (ELL) LP and teacher beliefs in California through an in-depth study of how two experienced bilingual teachers implemented reform. She found that teachers have agency to adapt policy to fit their ideological viewpoint. Similarly, Evans and Hornberger (2005) explored the legislation in No Child Left Behind (NCLB) pertaining to ELLs and how it was subsequently interpreted and (not) used at each additional metaphorical layer of LP implementation. Among their many findings, they revealed that teachers who had strong beliefs in the efficacy of their ELL pedagogy said they would not change anything in their local classroom language policies regardless of national policy, state demands and district requirements. In this book, we will demonstrate how teachers had varying degrees of agency connected to their school LP context, personal identities, lived experiences and teaching history, and how this resulted in very different DLBE implementation outcomes ranging from implementing the DLBE model with fidelity to abandoning the DLBE initiative altogether.

Language Ecology, Language as Practice and Social Theory

The framework or model is only half of what is needed to examine teachers' instructional choices embedded within multiple intersecting layers of LP; we also need an adequate theory. Thus, we combine an integrative LP framework with a language ecology perspective to open spaces to interpret micro LP in the context of macro LP and simultaneously attend to the complexities of language diversity.

In contrast to a diffusion-of-English paradigm that supports the spread of English for the economic gain of English speakers and English-speaking countries, an ecology of language perspective promotes and illuminates the preservation and diversification of languages (Hornberger, 2002; Phillipson & Skutnabb-Kangas, 1996). A pluralist language approach is a viable, present and active alternative to the one-nation-one-language standpoint (Hornberger, 2002). We build from the assumption that linguistic diversity is positive, and that diverse language practices are valuable for communities including school and classroom communities.

Aligned with a language ecology perspective, we embrace an understanding of language as practice. A useful metaphor is to think of language as a verb rather than a noun. Scholarship in applied linguistics and related fields (e.g. sociolinguistics, linguistic anthropology) increasingly challenges the traditional Saussurean view that languages are bounded systems of communication (think nouns) by reframing language as practice – in other words, as a form of action that emerges within particular social and cultural contexts (García, 2009a; Gutiérrez & Rogoff, 2003; Makoni & Pennycook, 2005; Pennycook, 2010). For example, in a DLBE program implementation, students are navigating and learning new language practices to engage socially with different people (initially English-dominant classmates, initially Spanish-dominant classmates, teachers, administrators) in different cultural contexts (cafeteria, playground, English classroom instruction, Spanish classroom instruction) all within a specific cultural institution (school) that has a whole set of linguistic and social norms and expectations that will differ in subtle or drastic ways from their home and/or community. By adopting an understanding of language as practice, the DLBE teacher's role for language instruction is much more complex than simply teaching 'English' or 'Spanish'; the DLBE teacher must equip students with as many linguistic tools and practices as possible to interact with a range of people across social and cultural contexts.

Such a radical reframing of language implies a need to rethink our notions of bilingualism. If languages are not bounded entities, then bilingualism must be more than simply the combination of two separate linguistic systems. García and Kleifgen (2010) propose a *dynamic bilingualism*, in which bilingualism is better understood as a repertoire of related language practices or ways of using language within particular sociocultural contexts. *Translanguaging* refers to the language practices and meaning-making processes of bilinguals. Most importantly, by adopting a view of language as practice, dynamic bilingualism and translanguaging, we ideologically embrace these practices as valid and valuable (García, 2009a). Students' complex bilingual practices or translanguaging offer cognitive and academic benefits on many levels (García, 2009a; García & Kleyn, 2016; Martínez, 2010; Palmer *et al.*, 2014).

To explore the language practices, including production and interaction, of teachers and students within DLBE classrooms, the investigation also draws on talk and social theory posited by Erickson (2004) to support our LP and language ecology frameworks. Erickson (2004) theorized that language practices are informed by non-local and prior processes, and we can explore connections between micro local language practices and macro societal processes:

> Thus I conclude by restating as a best guess the two truths we have been considering, propositions which I believe must necessarily be held together in a tension of paradox: (1) the conduct of talk in local social interaction as it occurs in real time is unique, crafted by local actors for the specific situation of its use in the moment of its uttering, and (2) the conduct of talk in local social interaction is profoundly influenced by processes that occur beyond the temporal and spatial horizon of the immediate occasion of interaction. (Erickson, 2004: 197)

Erickson argues that macro and micro processes work together in tension: shifts or changes are introduced and enacted simultaneously both from the top down and bottom up in what he terms the 'structure' and 'wiggle room' (e.g. agency) in local language ecologies.

Erickson's theory complements the LP framework which similarly aims to make connections across layers or levels of implementation. Thus, the combination of the LP 'onion' framework, a language ecology perspective with an understanding of language as practice and Erickson's assertion that 'macro' and 'micro' processes must be considered together, provided us with the tools for an in-depth analysis of local LP in the classrooms of focus in the following chapters. Teachers, we posit, are active language policymakers, taking advantage of that 'wiggle room' that Erickson describes.

Teachers as Language Policymakers

Teachers represent the center of the LP 'onion'; they are ultimately the brokers of any LP in the classroom (Hornberger & Johnson, 2011; Ricento & Hornberger, 1996), and increasing attention has been paid in recent research to their central role in both creating and implementing LP in schools and classrooms (Hornberger & Johnson, 2007; Johnson, 2010; Menken & García, 2010; Skilton-Sylvester, 2003; Stritikus & Garcia, 2000). The emphasis on the role of local practitioners in determining LP is a relatively recent phenomenon. Historical approaches in LP prior to the 1970s focused on language planning with little or no attention to the actual impact it had on practices (Hornberger, 2006). These approaches worked from a number of assumptions, including the idea that monolingualism or a language of wider communication is the ideal for social and economic development and the idea that language planning is a rational and objective activity (Fishman, 1969; Ricento, 2006). Language planning entailed developing a standard grammar and dictionary for languages that did not already have them, which was generally only necessary for indigenous or non-dominant languages in countries making LP decisions based on factors other than operational efficiency (Fishman, 1969; Haugen, 1959). Overall, linguists were concerned with trying to solve the 'language problem' in nation building particularly in developing countries (Ricento, 2000). As such, researchers did not attend to or even consider local actors.

Substantial research reinforces a LP framework that places local actors at the center; teachers have been identified extensively as critical language policymakers (Hornberger & Johnson, 2007; Johnson, 2010;

Menken & García, 2010; Skilton-Sylvester, 2003; Stritikus & Garcia, 2000). For example, Skilton-Sylvester (2003) explored macro and micro LP processes and their effects on Khmer language and literacy development; she found that local teacher policy can contest subtractive, macro-level legal discourse and decisions. Similarly, Varghese and Stritikus (2005) identified the critical role of teachers in LP through a cross-case study of bilingual teachers in two states. The authors argued that teachers, particularly teachers of ELLs, must be more educated and informed through teacher education on the role and impact of LP. The cases presented in this book build on this body of research, centering the role of the teacher to examine the implementation of DLBE programs and the classroom language practices that ultimately make up local LP.

Language Ideologies

Language ideologies – beliefs about language – and the implementation of LP cannot easily be separated; LP is ideological in nature. Hornberger (2002) described the implementation process of multilingual LP in Bolivia and South Africa as an effort to 'implement an ideology'. She highlighted the challenge of these implementation efforts in light of conflicting local ideologies, namely the priority to learn the dominant or national language (Hornberger, 2002). Similar insights have been made about LP in the United States. Researchers identified language-as-a-problem or assimilationist language ideologies in US federal LP, in particular Title III of the No Child Left Behind Act (NCLB) (Evans & Hornberger, 2005). For example, in 2001 with the adoption of *No Child Left Behind*, the section of federal law that pertained to 'limited English proficient' students changed from the previous law's (Elementary and Secondary Education Act [ESEA]) Title VII 'Bilingual Education Act' (BEA) to Title III's 'English Language Acquisition, Language Enhancement, and Academic Achievement Act'. Eliminating the word 'bilingual' and emphasizing English acquisition represents a subtractive, assimilationist ideology (Evans & Hornberger, 2005). In contrast, DLBE programs, whose goals are biliteracy and bilingualism, have been identified as representing an additive or pluralist ideology (García, 2009a).

Not surprisingly then, researchers exploring teachers as local policy agents often address and attend to teachers' ideologies. Valdiviezo (2009) investigated the role of teachers in bilingual education policy implementation in Peru, finding that teachers' beliefs were essential in both the reproduction and contestation of systematic inequalities. Gkaintartzi and Tsokalidou (2011) explored the micro-level ideologies of four teachers in mainstream Greek schools through semi-structured interviews and observations. They found that teachers' responses could be placed on a continuum ranging from awareness of the importance of bilingualism and minority language maintenance to the absolute rejection of the minority language and the subtraction of bilingualism. Furthermore, a teacher's language ideologies are not necessarily aligned with their classroom language practices. Karathanos (2009) explored US mainstream teachers' perspectives on the use of the home language in instruction and found that teachers who generally supported first language (L1) use in instruction tended to show stronger support for its underlying theory than for its practical implementation.

Because we will be exploring teachers' experiences in the implementation of a top-down mandated DLBE LP, we will consider the role of language ideologies at multiple levels. It is thus critical for the framing of this project to be clear about how language ideologies are defined. We will briefly describe the ways in which the concept of ideology and language ideology has been used historically before addressing how we use it in this book specifically.

Given the complexity of language ideology as a concept, it is helpful to break the term apart and first explore definitions of *ideology*. Ideology is a multifaceted concept theorized by numerous scholars. According to Apple (1990: 18), people generally agree that ideology refers to 'some sort of "system" of ideas, beliefs, fundamental commitments, or values about social reality'. Eagleton (1991), however, argues that it is unproductive to conceive of any single definition; rather, competing definitions of ideology have been and are useful for different purposes. Eagleton (1991: 1–2) provides a list of 15 distinct working definitions, including 'the process of production of meanings, signs and values in social life', 'forms of thoughts motivated by social interests', 'ideas which help to legitimate a dominant political power' and 'identity thinking'. Some of the definitions are not compatible with one another; nevertheless, power and legitimization emerge as central issues in most of Eagleton's definitions of ideology.

Woolard (1998) provides an alternative perspective. She identifies four common strands: (a) ideology as dealing with consciousness; (b) ideology as connected to a particular social position; (c) ideology as connected to power; and (d) ideology as a power-laden distortion. Woolard recognizes a split between the second and third strands, moving from a more 'neutral' to a negative view of ideology, acknowledging that scholars draw on both forms within the field of anthropology.

Interestingly, the possible definitions of *language* ideology tend to mirror the debates about defining ideology in general. Indeed, the use of *language ideologies* in contrast to *ideology* should not imply a narrowing conceptualization of ideology (Woolard, 1998). Despite wide variation in scholarship on language ideologies, there is a consensus that language ideologies are not just about language (Woolard, 1998).

The concept of language ideologies has been most frequently used as an analytical tool in the field of linguistic anthropology, a hybrid field combining linguistics and sociocultural anthropology. Within this strand of research, scholars tend to be concerned with how sets of beliefs about language impact social interactions, social relations and speech patterns. Lippi-Green (1997), for example, examined the privileging or oppressing of distinct language practices through the myth of language 'standardization'. Another interest of linguistic anthropologists has been examining *embodied* language ideologies in a speech community. Kroskrity (1998) explored language ideology in Arizona Tewa speech, finding that community members embodied kiva talk (the speech performed in religious ceremonies) in multiple naturalized ways to collectively serve as a dominant language ideology in the speech community. In these cases, it is evident how linguistic anthropologists have used the construct of language ideology to go beyond individual beliefs about language to explore how collectively shared assumptions and embodiments of beliefs function in society.

Indeed, Kroskrity (1998: 117) critiqued the study of language ideology at a solely metalinguistic level: 'Any rethinking of language ideology that would exclude naturalized, dominant ideologies and thus analytically segregate beliefs about language according to a criterion of consciousness seems to me to be unwise'. Kroskrity (1998) argued for a more complex, multifaceted understanding of language ideology: a definition that encompasses a larger scope.

Let's examine the scope and relation to power of the language ideology concept across three definitions from scholars in the field of linguistic anthropology. The first seminal definition, from Silverstein (1979: 202), is a 'set of beliefs about language articulated by users as a rationalization or justification of perceived language structure and use'. We would argue that this definition of language ideology is limited in scope; the word 'articulated' implies some form of speaker awareness or consciousness. The words 'rationalization' and 'justification' connect the concept with power, specifically the use of language to serve group interests, yet these two words also imply a level of consciousness that we have found is not always present.

A second definition of language ideology comes from Kroskrity (2004: 498): 'beliefs, or feelings, about languages as used in their social worlds'.

This conceptualization is greater in scope than Silverstein's, because the word 'used' allows for a multiplicity of potential practices. A language ideology, according to Kroskrity's definition, could operate consciously or unconsciously and it could be used to silence, empower or oppress. With respect to power, this definition is not limited to uses that serve the dominant group in power, although it implies that these beliefs or feelings about languages are being used for some kind of societal interest.

Finally, Woolard (1998: 3) defines language ideologies as 'representations, whether explicit or implicit, that construe the intersection of language and human beings in a social world'. This definition is broadest in scope. The word 'representations' can include spoken, embodied or symbolic manifestations. The phrase 'explicit or implicit' attends to the issue of consciousness and encapsulates expressions at all levels of awareness. This definition appears to de-center the issue of power by including all ways that language and human beings can intersect rather than limiting us, as the others do, to the ways language ideologies are 'used' or 'rationalized'.

As Eagleton (1991) argued, competing definitions of ideology are useful for different purposes; the same is true for different conceptualizations of language ideology. For various reasons, from here on out we will primarily reference Kroskrity's (2004: 498) definition of language ideology: 'beliefs, or feelings, about languages as used in their social worlds'. This definition serves us as a dependable construct we find we can use as an analytic tool; it is not too narrow in scope to be limiting and not too abstract to become diffuse.

This conception of language ideology serves our needs because it allows for 'uses' that are potentially hegemonic, counter-hegemonic (or both) as well as multiple and contradictory. Research exposes the multiple and contradictory nature of language ideologies. These inconsistencies can occur within a community of speakers. For example, Hill (1998) explored nostalgia expressed by Mexicano (Nahuatl) speakers as an ideological discourse. She found that while the nostalgia discourse was prevalent among older, high-status males and younger males who worked outside of the community, women did not participate in the discourse. Rather, women engaged in oppositional discourses by addressing the nostalgia discourse and providing counter narratives or pointing out its paradoxical nature. The contradictions can also occur within an individual speaker. For example, Martínez (2013) explored the language ideologies of California middle school students toward Spanglish. When asked about their hybrid language practices, his participants would initially and frequently provide a deficit rationale that indicated the students' internalization of the dominant language ideology. However, upon closer examination, Martínez found instances of students adopting what he called counter-hegemonic language ideologies: they asserted at various moments that Spanglish was normal, sounded better and enabled cultural maintenance. Similarly, Martínez *et al.* (2014) found that two DLBE teachers' perspectives about translanguaging simultaneously reflected both ideologies of linguistic purism and counter-hegemonic ideologies valuing bilingualism. The teacher cases presented in Chapters 4–6 will demonstrate both multiplicity and contradiction in teachers' articulated and embodied language ideologies.

Given that we will be paying attention to the language ideologies of teachers implementing a DLBE program, the space in this definition for potential counter-hegemonic ideologies is crucial. Arguably, DLBE programs represent a counter-hegemonic pluralist ideology in the context of a more dominant assimilationist ideology in the United States at large (de Jong, 2011; Freeman, 2004; Lindholm-Leary, 2001). As such, the ways in which teachers' language ideologies, both articulated and embodied, align or misalign (or both) with the program's intended ideologies might have important implications for classroom LP. This understanding of language ideologies provides the space to critically examine these kinds of multiplicity and contradiction.

As we specifically consider certain articulations and embodiments of language ideology in schools, de Jong's (2013) distinction between assimilationist and pluralist discourse serves as an important analytic tool to make sense of the teachers' multiple language ideologies and their (mis)alignment with LP. Assimilationist and pluralist discourses represent distinct perspectives on the value of language diversity, the view of bilinguals, the preferred program model and policy into practice (see de Jong, 2013: 99). On the one hand, viewing monolingualism as the norm, seeing language variety as a problem, understanding bilingualism from a fractional standpoint and supporting English-only or transitional bilingual programs for emergent bilingual students are all perspectives that index an *assimilationist* discourse. On the other hand, viewing multilingualism as the norm, seeing linguistic diversity as positive, understanding bilingualism from a holistic standpoint and supporting DLBE or other enrichment-oriented bilingual programs index a *pluralist* discourse. We draw on de Jong's ideological distinction as a framework to unpack teachers articulated and embodied language ideologies.

Kroskrity's definition is also a good one for our analysis because he conceives of language ideology as an active process. He places less emphasis on the beliefs themselves (noun) and more on the *uses* of the beliefs (verb). As we share teachers' cases in the following chapters, we will identify the language ideologies they articulate as well as how they then embody or 'use' these ideologies as local LP. Fortunately, using the concept of language ideologies as an analytic lens has particular affordances. As Gal (1998: 319) explained, 'By starting with linguistic ideologies, one can highlight unexpected links, contestations, and contradictions among such organizations, thereby bringing them within a single theoretical purview'. Thus, we will explore teachers' language ideologies in the context of DLBE program implementation in a large urban school district, which has multiple layers including district implementation, school implementation and teacher implementation (Hornberger & Johnson, 2007). We will identify tensions and pull apart and make connections between the distinct layers.

Furthermore, language ideology as an analytic tool can capture wide variation. Kroskrity (2004: 496) states, 'It is more useful to have an analytic device which captures diversity rather than emphasizing a static, uniformly shared culture'. As it happens, in selecting our teacher cases to highlight, we have worked to maximize variation. This has helped us to capture a surprisingly vast spread of differences in practices, processes and beliefs within and across classrooms in this single district.

Finally, Gal (1998) offers another provocative reason for placing such emphasis on ideologies:

> Language ideologies are doubly significant... because they participate in the semiotic processes through which ideas become naturalized, essentialized, universalized, or commonsensical; ideas about language are implicated in the process by which *any* cultural ideas gain the discursive authority to become dominant. (Gal, 1998: 321–322)

If we consider the classroom as a local site capable of forming its own dominant ideology, teachers' ideologies become 'doubly significant'. Not only do they impact local LP, but they also filter all of the cultural ideas in the classroom: curriculum, instruction, community, etc., are all filtered through the lens of these local dominant ideologies. This, we argue, should matter to people at every level of education.

Dual Language Bilingual Education Program Implementation

The potential success of a DLBE program is contingent on its implementation. Prior research identifies multiple factors and potential challenges for DLBE program implementation (Freeman, 2004; Howard, Sugarman *et al.*, 2003; Howard *et al.*, 2018; Lindholm-Leary, 2001). Practical implementation issues include having sufficient materials, sufficient professional development or DLBE training, adequate DLBE curriculum and a suitable student population (Lindholm-Leary, 2001). A unique aspect of the study out of which these cases emerged was its focus on top-down, large-scale implementation of DLBE programs. Wright (2004) posits that top-down LP mandates are often motivated for political reasons rather than practical; for this reason, they can lack essential resources and funding.

A strong program model is also identified as crucial for DLBE implementation. Lindholm-Leary (2001) identifies the features of a strong DLBE program model including: four to six years duration, exposure to optimal dual language input, constant language output opportunities, minimum 50% of instruction in target language and literacy instruction in both languages. With regard to the division of language of instruction, the two most common models are 90-10 and 50-50. Both of these models have been associated with high academic achievement (Collier & Thomas, 2004; Gómez *et al.*, 2005) and, as described in Chapter 1, the district under investigation in this study implemented the Gómez-Gómez 50/50 model.

An additional controversial feature that Lindholm-Leary (2001) advocates is the strict separation of languages for instruction, as discussed in Chapter 1. This is the idea that teachers should teach (and in some cases, students should be expected to engage) in either one target language or the other; languages should not be mixed. Indeed, according to Lindholm-Leary (2001), the successful implementation of DLBE programs requires 'fidelity to the model', which includes language separation. Advocates of the strict separation of languages in DLBE programs contend that this is necessary for the protection of the minority language and for optimal language acquisition (Cloud *et al.*, 2000; Howard & Sugarman, 2007). Meanwhile, recent scholarship questions the artificiality and ultimately the usefulness of separating languages for emergent bilingual students. Drawing on a long history of research in linguistics demonstrating that language mixing is a normal and natural practice for bilinguals (e.g. MacSwan & Faltis, 2019; Urciuoli, 1995; Zentella, 1997), scholars and educators are beginning to theorize new ways to engage in language and content integrated learning in bilingual contexts – most recently called translanguaging pedagogies – that won't marginalize bilingual language practices (García, 2009a; García & Kleyn, 2016; Palmer & Martínez, 2013; Palmer, Martínez *et al.*, 2014; Reyes, 2001). At this point, however, DLBE programs are still primarily embedded within a language separation paradigm, and the program model that our focal district adopted advocated the separation of languages by content area.

One complication for DLBE program implementation is the current sociopolitical emphasis on standardized testing for accountability in public schools. The additive goals of DLBE – bilingualism, biculturalism and biliteracy – can conflict with accountability pressure to perform well on monolingual exams (Henderson & Palmer, 2015b; Palmer, Henderson, Wall, Zuñiga & Berthelsen, 2015; Pérez, 2004). Teachers become the key local language policymakers to negotiate this tension, and teachers can feel obligated to dedicate time to test preparation, taking away from content instruction (Pérez, 2004). At the same time, school communities have been known to draw on their standardized test scores to provide legitimacy and advocate for ongoing support of their DLBE programs (Pérez, 2004).

The successful implementation of DLBE programs requires more than fulfilling practical programmatic needs (Calderón & Minaya-Rowe, 2003; Cloud *et al.*, 2000; Howard & Sugarman, 2007; Lindholm-Leary, 2001). Lindholm-Leary's (2001) comprehensive review of the necessary features for DLBE implementation included, in addition to the aforementioned features, system-wide and even ideological aspects that require broad and deep investment. For example, she recommended effective leadership, which includes administrative support (at every level) and educators throughout schools who are knowledgeable about the program's goals and features; she also asserted the need for a conducive school environment, which she defined as a positive and additive bilingual environment, a reciprocal instructional style and educators with cross-cultural competence. Similarly, Howard and Sugarman (2007) assert that the successful implementation of DLBE programs requires more than a strong model:

> On their own, program models, curricula, and instructional strategies are necessary but insufficient means to achieve the goals of academic achievement, bilingualism and biliteracy, and cross-cultural competence in two-way immersion (dual language). Unless the program fosters empowerment and demonstrates respect for students, staff, and parents through cultures of intellectualism, equity, and leadership, good design alone will not lead to good outcomes for student achievement. (Howard & Sugarman, 2007: 10)

This point illustrates the need for a high degree of investment in a DLBE program by different stakeholders at all levels of implementation. Calderón and Minaya-Rowe (2003) echo this, arguing for the importance of sharing information among stakeholders in the planning and designing of two-way DLBE implementation. At the implementation stage, the authors highlight the need for effective DLBE curriculum and instruction and parent involvement. The necessary attributes identified by these researchers highlight the complicated and multifaceted nature of the 'successful' implementation of DLBE programs.

Not surprisingly, language ideologies matter in the complex process of implementing DLBE programs (Cummins, 2000; Freeman, 1998, 2004; Palmer, 2011; Palmer, Henderson *et al.*, 2015; Pérez, 2004; Stritikus, 2003; Varghese, 2008). Ideological multiplicity at the school level can be a challenge for DLBE implementation. In her study of two DLBE programs in Texas, Pérez (2004) found that parent and educator ideologies were contradictory and complicated throughout the implementation process. Dominant language ideologies can, in fact, interfere with DLBE program implementation. Freeman (1998) explored DLBE implementation at a two-way dual language school in Washington, DC, and found that the competing ideologies between the additive school discourse and subtractive societal discourse appeared to make it impossible for the DLBE implementation to achieve its full pluralist vision. Although the teachers at the school worked hard to create what she termed 'alternative discourses' that would engage pluralist ideologies and center bilingualism as an asset, English dominance seeped into the classroom. Freeman (2004) came to a similar conclusion years later following a separate investigation of LP and DLBE program implementation in Philadelphia. She described the role of language ideologies: 'Local language ideologies strongly influence the ease with which a language plan can be effectively developed and implemented' (Freeman, 2004: 81). She re-emphasized how the (dis)congruency of a program's ideological assumptions with the local language ideologies will impact program implementation.

Indeed, Freeman (2004: 82) argued for what she viewed as the central issue for implementing the DLBE program: 'The real challenge is destabilizing established language ideologies and replacing them with alternative language ideologies'. Following this argument, Freeman appealed to local educators including administrators, parents, and teachers to be active in creating new LP in line with the ideological underpinnings of additive programs. Other researchers have echoed these findings in a range of US contexts, all in Spanish-English two-way DLBE programs: middle-class English-speaking students dominated the discourse in a second-grade classroom in California, despite the classroom teacher's ongoing efforts (Palmer, 2009); teachers' standard language ideologies dominated in a middle school, marginalizing speakers of non-standard varieties of either language (McCollum, 1994); English took over children's interaction in a kindergarten classroom, seemingly regardless of their home language preferences and skills (DePalma, 2010); English became the language of social interaction in a fifth-grade class in Illinois (Potowski, 2004).

It seems to us that the complexity of ideologies for both individuals and communities, nested within the complexity of implementing DLBE programs, deserves fuller attention. One of our aims in gathering together in one place the range of teacher cases from across this diverse urban district is to extend previous work on DLBE to interrogate and explore our understanding of the role of language ideologies within the program implementation process. We need a more complete and complex understanding of the ways ideologies work at the local level in interaction with dominant even hegemonic ideologies if educators are to be equipped with strategies to disrupt them. We hope this exploration contributes both theoretically and practically in this direction.

Summary

Research on DLBE implementation demonstrates it is a multifaceted process in which language ideologies play a role in constructing local LP that values and promotes linguistic diversity. In sum, the following theories and assumptions guide and frame the DLBE teacher cases we present in this book:

- LP includes multiple, intersecting layers (i.e. onion) with different stakeholders impacting implementation at each level.
- Teachers are at the heart of the LP onion and are understood as key language policymakers who negotiate and interpret multiple, intersecting layers of LP.
- Linguistic diversity is positive and diverse language practices are valuable for the language ecology of communities including schools and classrooms.
- Language is a practice that is both crafted by local actors and influenced by macro social processes.
- Language ideologies are beliefs about language that are used in social worlds, which includes 'uses' that are hegemonic, counter-hegemonic or both.
- Language ideologies are multiple and contradictory and can reflect pluralist or assimilationist discourse.
- Language ideologies are articulated and embodied and influence local LP.

3 Teacher Perspectives on a District-Wide Dual Language Bilingual Education Language Policy Implementation: An Overview

Before we delve into the particulars of the individual teachers who will make up the remainder of this book, we want to share methodology details about the larger study from which these data emerged and provide an overview of the findings from the district-wide study. In the first part of this chapter, we will present the context of the study, the participants and an overview of our data collection and analysis. In the second part of the chapter, we explore how the educators working across the district in the over 60 dual language bilingual education (DLBE) programs district-wide described and evaluated their experience with top-down mandated DLBE policy implementation, and what implementation issues they identified as important. This chapter serves to provide context and background information to understand the teacher cases presented in Chapters 4–6.

Part 1: Context of the Study and Methodology

The research undergirding this book took place over a four-year period in a large urban school district in Texas. In 2009, just prior to the beginning of this study, the district served a total of approximately 80,000 students of which approximately 25% were labeled as 'limited English proficient' (i.e. emergent bilinguals) and 50% economically disadvantaged. The district reported its own demographic as approximately 50% Hispanic, 30% white, 10% African American, 5% Asian and the remaining 5% predominantly two or more races. Although a few prior efforts had been made to initiate DLBE programs in the district, none had lasted longer than a few years for various reasons (primarily account-ability pressures). In 2009, no schools were offering DLBE in the district. Approximately 60 schools offered transitional bilingual education, in compliance with Texas Education Code (Chapter 89).

The district decision-making process

Within the current high-stakes accountability systems in the United States, pressure on districts is extreme to continue to improve academic success as measured by standardized tests for increasingly diverse popula-tions of students. In this large urban school district in Texas, as in many such districts, emergent bilingual students are among the lowest-scoring students on state and federal accountability measures, and as their num-bers increase so increases the risk of negative consequences to their school campuses and even threats of job loss to the teachers and principals who serve them.

In August 2009, a new superintendent came into the district and immediately began to ask why the district did not have DLBE programs, which she framed as an obvious solution to their accountability issues with low-scoring bilingual students. With the vocal support of enthusi-astic (largely middle-class) parents, teachers and community members, she convinced the school board to approve a 'Dual Language Initiative' in December 2010. The executive director of bilingual education and English as a second language (ESL) programs, a district-level administra-tor, was charged with finding and implementing an appropriate DLBE program model for the district. Drs Leo and Richard Gómez won the district's contract, in part because their program came as a full pack-age, complete with teacher training and supporting arguments based on accountability rhetoric. The Gómez-Gómez team promised improved academic outcomes for English language learner (ELL) students across the board, pointing to their own successes in South Texas (Gómez *et al.*, 2005) and citing the large-scale national research study carried out by Virginia Collier and Wayne Thomas (2004).

Implementation began in the winter of 2010 with a campus applica-tion and selection process for 10 'pilot' campuses (four two-way dual language and six one-way dual language), which would begin to imple-ment the program in August 2010. Subsequently, being one year ahead in their implementation process, these 10 campuses would serve as 'models' for the other 50 (or so) schools with bilingual education programs. All other district bilingual campuses would begin the program in August 2011. Most administrators and teachers associated with the pilot schools received their training in late spring and summer 2010.

Campuses interested in being considered for the pilot year were required to make the case for their selection as model campuses for DLBE program implementation, submitting evidence of specific eligibility requirements including Title I status (required because of the district's plan for funding the programs), strong leadership invested in bilingual programming, parent and teacher support for the implementation and available space on the campus for expansion (particularly important for campuses seeking to adopt the two-way model). A committee of school district stakeholders, including community members, parents, teachers and district administrators, convened to examine the submitted applications and select the schools. As a university professor in bilingual education, Deb (Author 2) served on this committee, and continued to serve on an advisory committee for dual language education for the district throughout the years of implementation.

Our research team, meanwhile, began with a focus on one of the pilot campuses implementing a two-way DLBE program: a small Title I school near the center of the city, situated in a rapidly gentrifying neighborhood but serving a community that at that time was 95% Latinx, approximately 80% of whom carried the English learner (EL) label. In Year 2, with the support of our colleague Shannon Fitzsimmons-Doolan, we carried out a district-wide survey of educators at DLBE campuses (Fitzsimmons-Doolan *et al.*, 2015). In Year 3 of the study, focusing on third-grade teachers and classrooms, we expanded to include a second pilot campus, slightly larger, also serving a predominantly Latinx community. In Year 4, Katy (Author 1) carried out interviews with educators throughout the district and observed in three purposively selected classrooms. The case studies in this book came out of these different stages of the study (Table 3.1).

Participants and data collection

This book draws on data from four years of research in a large urban school district in Texas that was implementing district-wide DLBE; we were involved in data collection from 2010 through 2014. The larger study involved several year-long sub-studies, all exploring related questions about the implementation of DLBE. In Year 1 (2010–2011), along with Suzanne García-Mateus and Will Slade, we carried out an ethnography and discourse analysis of policy implementation at one small school (Nuñez & Palmer, 2017; Palmer, 2020; Palmer, Henderson *et al.*, 2015). In Year 2 (2011–2012), a team that included Nancy Roser and several additional colleagues in the fields of early childhood education and language and literacy, carried out an exploration of the development of critical literacies in primary grades with the introduction of process drama and multicultural children's literature (García-Mateus & Palmer, 2017; Palmer, Martínez *et al.*, 2014; Roser, Martínez, Moore & Palmer, 2015; Roser, Palmer, Greeter, Martinez & Wooten, 2015). In Year 3 (2012–2013), with several other colleagues including Dorothy Wall, Christian Zúñiga and Stefan Berthelsen, we observed the planning and practice of teams of third-grade teachers in two small schools as they negotiated the implementation of both the DLBE program and the State of Texas Assessments of Academic Readiness (STAAR) statewide high-stakes standardized testing (Henderson & Palmer, 2015b; Palmer, Henderson *et al.*, 2015; Palmer & Henderson, 2016). As previously mentioned, in Year 3, we carried out a district-wide survey of educators' language ideologies with our colleague Shannon Fitzsimmons-Doolan (Fitzsimmons-Doolan *et al.*, 2015). Katy then followed up and interviewed 20 of the survey participants, and collected observational field note data in three of their classrooms in Year 4 (2013–2014). At the same time (also in Year 4), our close collaborator Suzanne García-Mateus closed out the data collection for her four-year longitudinal study on the development of bilingualism and biliteracy of six focal children who began the program along with us in 2010. For all of these studies, we were primary collaborators but certainly not the sole contributors.

Altogether, our team collected several hundred hours of audio-video recordings of classroom interactions in pre-K through Grade 5 DLBE classrooms over the course of four years at several schools throughout the district. We interviewed approximately 30 educators (20 as part of Katy's data collection in Year 4, and the others as part of the ethnographic studies carried out in Years 1 and 3). We collected field notes in classrooms, planning sessions, parent–teacher meetings, professional development sessions, school- and district-level administrative meetings and in the everyday workings of the school and district throughout the process of implementation in these first three years. We drew on our experiences throughout the various stages of the study in writing this book.

One of our case study teachers, Olivia (Chapter 6), from Hillside, was part of the first-year ethnography of implementation (Year 1, 2010–2011). Katy collected over 20 hours of audio/video data in Olivia's classroom during the fall of 2010 and spring 2011, and we carried out two semi-structured interviews with her; Deb spoke to her in August and Katy spoke to her in November (Henderson & Palmer, 2015b).

Two of the case study teachers, Rachel (Chapter 4) and Lisel (Chapter 5), both third-grade teachers at Woodward Elementary, were part of our third-grade high-stakes accountability study, carried out in Year 3 (2012–2013), in which we sought to understand how teams of third-grade teachers negotiated the policy discord between the introduction of

Table 3.1 District-wide DLBE implementation study: Four-year overview of research

School year	Study	Data collected	Publications
Year 1 2010–2011	First-year ethnography of implementation of DLBE in 'one small school' – August through December	Ten interviews of educators and leaders Ethnographic field notes throughout school Audio/video recordings of interactions in DLBE classrooms	Palmer (2020) Henderson & Palmer (2015a) Nuñez & Palmer (2017) Palmer, Henderson *et al.* (2015)
Year 2 2011–2012	Process drama literacy study	Interview with four first-grade and second-grade teachers Video recordings of lessons related to drama and multicultural children's literature	Roser, Martinez *et al.* (2015); Roser, Palmer *et al.* (2015) Palmer *et al.* (2014) García-Mateus & Palmer (2018)
Year 3 2012–2013	District-wide mixed-methods survey study	Survey (Fitzsimmons-Doolan, 2011) with qualitative questions added, carried out with random sample of 323 educators in DLBE schools throughout district	Fitzsimmons-Doolan *et al.* (2015)
Year 3 2012–2013	Third-grade high-stakes accountability and DLBE study	Field notes from weekly third-grade team planning meetings at two schools Interviews of four TW DLBE third-grade teachers Field notes of interactions in two third-grade classrooms	Palmer, Henderson *et al.* (2015) Henderson & Palmer (2015b) Palmer & Henderson (2016)
Year 4 2013–2014	Interviews/ observations to explore dual language bilingual education, language ideologies and local language policy	Twenty teacher interviews and follow-up classroom observations of three teachers selected based on variation in language ideological orientation	Henderson (2015, 2017, 2020)

high-stakes standardized testing and the implementation of DLBE (Henderson & Palmer, 2015b; Palmer & Henderson, 2016; Palmer, Henderson *et al.*, 2015). Katy took field notes and audio-recorded these teachers' team planning meetings (with four teachers present) for 18 sessions throughout the year, interviewed each of the two two-way DLBE teachers once at the beginning of the school year and spent approximately 10 hours in each two-way DLBE classroom taking detailed field notes and collecting approximately three hours of audio/video recorded student–teacher interactions.

The remainder of the teachers who we highlight as cases in the following chapters, as well as the findings we report on in this chapter about district-wide language ideologies and implementation issues, were part of the district-wide survey (2012–2013) and Katy's dissertation study in which she carried out follow-up interviews and observations of willing participants (2013–2014). Each of these three teachers, Marisol (Chapter 4), Mariana (Chapter 5) and Michael (Chapter 6), filled out the *Educators' Beliefs about Language* survey, participated in a one-hour, follow-up, semi-structured interview, and then allowed Katy to spend time observing in his/her classroom, taking detailed field notes. Katy spent approximately 20 hours in each classroom.

The second part of this chapter will report on findings from two sources, collected in Years 3 and 4 of the larger study: the results of the survey (*Educators' Beliefs about Language*) of a random sample of 323 educators in the district (Fitzsimmons-Doolan *et al.*, 2015) and follow-up interviews conducted with 20 of those survey participants by Katy. The *Educators Beliefs about Language* survey had two sections with 50 items and was distributed with help from the district to a random sample of 1460 educators. Section 1 targeted educators' beliefs about language and Section 2 targeted educators' experiences with DLBE program implementation and personal background information. Section 1 was developed and tested for reliability and validity by Shannnon Fitzsimmons-Doolan (2011, 2014) and had been used prior to this study. From the original random sample, 381 participants began the survey (26% return rate) and 323 met the inclusion requirements: they agreed to participate, answered yes to working in a DLBE school and completed the first section of the survey. Respondents represented all of the district DLBE schools.

The final question on the *Educators' Beliefs about Language* survey asked whether or not the participant would be willing to be contacted for a follow-up interview. Of the 323 participants in the study, 115 agreed to be contacted. For the purposes of this study, the sample was further limited based on two criteria: (1) direct participation in the DLBE program; and (2) identification as 'teacher' (as opposed to administrator). Of the 115 educators willing to participate in the follow-up study, 43 participants met these additional two criteria and of those 43 potential participants, 20 were interviewed. Table 3.2 lists the interview participants by pseudonym, grade level, years of experience, language, gender and age.

Participants chose to complete the interview in English or in Spanish; approximately 50% of the participants chose to do so in each language. Interviews were semi-structured and guided by an interview protocol that asked open-ended questions about teachers' beliefs about language and experiences with DLBE implementation (Patton, 2002). The data presented in this chapter focus on the teachers' responses to questions about DLBE policy and implementation.

Table 3.2 Participants

Pseudonym	Grade level	Years teaching	Language	Gender	Age
Maria	Pre-K	9	English	Female	34
Irene	Pre-K	5	Bilingual	Female	52
Berta	Pre-K	12	Bilingual	Female	56
Marisol	Pre-K	8	Bilingual	Female	39
Sandra	Pre-K	5	Bilingual	Female	49
Jill	Pre-K	15	English	Female	59
Edward	K	20	Bilingual	Male	42
Susana	K	11	Bilingual	Female	52
Lucia	K	4	Bilingual	Female	27
Cathy	K	5	English	Female	33
Daniel	1st	1	Bilingual	Male	25
Gustavo	1st	N/A	Bilingual	Male	41
Chrissy	2nd	8	Bilingual	Female	48
Deina	2nd	3	Bilingual	Female	27
Samantha	2nd	15	English	Female	56
Mariana	3rd	9	Bilingual	Female	N/A
Tamy	3rd	17	English	Female	44
Michael	3rd	13	Bilingual	Male	37
Ramón	4th	6	Bilingual	Male	34
Uriel	4th	N/A	Bilingual	Male	54

Data analysis

Interview data were treated as both socially constructed narratives and potentially valid accounts of reality. We assumed that the perspective of the respondent was meaningful and knowable (Patton, 2002). Respondents were viewed as constantly engaging in knowledge making of their own and other's action (Emerson *et al.*, 2011). However, interviews were also treated, interpreted and analyzed as complex, social interactions; the data collected were partial and socially (co)constructed (Alvesson, 2003). Miller and Glassner (1997: 133) argued for this theoretical standpoint on interviews: 'While the interview is itself a symbolic interaction, this does not discount the possibility that knowledge of the social world beyond the interaction can be obtained'. We treated interview data as an accurate representation of teacher experience alongside careful consideration of how our social interaction with the teachers influenced what they did and did not say.

This project was in line with the reasoning that data do not exist objectively, and data analysis begins alongside data collection and infiltrates all points of the research process (Emerson *et al.*, 2011). Following each interview, we completed an analytic memo, which served as an early stage of analysis and informed thematic analysis. After data collection was completed, the interviews were transcribed and analyzed thematically (Miles & Huberman, 1994). A text analysis markup system (TAMS) analyzer was used for data management (Weinstein, 2012). A second coder increased coding reliability. The coding analysis was a multistep process. First, both coders read the first five interviews and independently generated a code list. We met to discuss our independent code lists to create an initial master code list. Next, we jointly coded two interviews. During this process, we discussed coding discrepancies and modified the master code list and code definitions, accordingly. We then went through three iterations of independent coding. After each independent coding, we met to further discuss, modify and negotiate the master code list. This coding process is depicted in Hruschka *et al.* (2004: 311). Discussion and analysis of discrepancies enabled deeper insight into the data. Collaboration in qualitative coding is particularly helpful for broader theoretical constructs (Collier & Thomas, 2004; Lindholm-Leary, 2001; Rolstad *et al.*, 2005; Silverman & Marvasti, 2008). In other words, multiple coders afforded the ability to member check and co-construct meaning.

The final master code list had 62 codes, 45 of which were global codes and could be applied anywhere over the course of the interview. This chapter presents the findings from the themes connected to DLBE language policy implementation.

Part 2: District-Wide Findings

District-wide data reflected a wide variation in teacher views on language and DLBE implementation. We first present the findings from the district-wide survey followed by DLBE teacher interviews. The district-wide survey data included a range of educators, not all of whom were teachers in the DLBE program. Both sections reveal variation in the investment in the DLBE program and issues of implementation identified by the participants.

Investment in DLBE across educators in the district

Across educators in the district, there was strong evidence for the presence of both assimilationist and pluralist ideologies as well as both rejection of and support for DLBE implementation.

The assimilationist comments stood out as incompatible ideologies with a DLBE enrichment model and implementation:

Aspects of this model are definitely not developmentally appropriate with regard to ELL's who come into the classroom at a deficit- the fundamentals are not in place.

When I lived in Spain, I was expected to speak Spanish. When I lived in Germany, I was expected to speak German... I learned to speak four different languages because that is what their countries spoke. I did not expect anyone to make any accommodations for me, it was my responsibility. This is the United States and our language is English.

I think it is important that if children are expected to speak English in an educational setting by the third or fourth grade they be given the opportunity to learn that language prior to these grades. I think it would be more beneficial to have Spanish speaking students follow the same ESL curriculum that other non-English speakers use, rather than be separated into a bilingual classroom. Students who enter PreK are entering during the language acquisition period and their brains will learn English easier than when they are older.

Collectively, the underlying ideologies embedded within these comments – including a deficit view of emerging bilingual (EB) students, a monolingual understanding of the United States, school as an English space and misconceptions of second language acquisition – represent roadblocks for local DLBE implementation. The increased difficulty and challenge for district-wide program implementation are readily transparent; teachers' personal investment in the program cannot be assumed.

Issues of DLBE implementation identified by educators across the district

Moving beyond initial program investment, survey analysis revealed a wide variation in educators' views concerning the amount of resources and professional development provided for them. Furthermore, assessment, intimately connected with grade level, similarly emerged as a constraint on the DLBE implementation process. One teacher succinctly wrote in her comment, 'The bottom line is to pass the test'. Additional themes identified as salient issues for the implementation process included the student population, a lack of local support (e.g. from administrators, parents, instructional coaches), teachers' misconceptions (about a range of things) and contradictions between and within district and local curriculum and program mandates. Two of the survey teachers' comments are presented to highlight this variation and provide a window into some of these issues:

> I understand the basis for the dual language program however I see a need for resources in Spanish for Science, Social Studies and Language Arts. Most of the resources needed for the lessons are in English. I'm referring to videos. The program is then tailored to the population of a campus, so the essence of the program is being tweaked. Due to these changes, not every campus is doing Dual Language the way it 'should be'. I think there's a lot the program needs to improve in order for it to 'work' across the district. The Dual Language conflicts with what the district wants and what the administration at the campus wants. It's hard for me as a teacher to meet everyone's needs on top of the student's needs. In order to implement this program correctly, there needs to be Tier [leveled support] trainings for everyone.

> I love the Dual Language Program. I am not sure about the implementation. Sometimes I receive conflicting information depending on who I am talking to (the district or the Gómez and Gómez people). The conflicts are usually minor such as the ratio of Spanish to English activities in the bilingual centers. I feel I was given lots of resources and information by my fellow teammates who have taught the program before, [and by] administration at my school and the district.

These comments provide insight into a range of issues. In the first comment, the teacher recognized the purpose of DLBE, but identified the availability of materials and support, and general 'fidelity to the model', as problems in the way of effective implementation. Additional professional development is recognized as a possible solution; however, the contradictions between what the district wants and what local administration wants remained an obstacle. In the second comment, there is immediate tension between theoretically supporting the model and the local messy reality of implementing it. In contrast to the sentiment expressed in the first comment, this teacher expresses feeling adequately supported with resources; however, they still struggle with contradictory policy messages. In both comments, we can see the different layers of language policy intersecting.

Issues with the model often intersected with educator misconceptions and language ideologies, as illustrated with these two comments:

> I feel that the Dual Language program is excellent for some students (those already naturally gifted linguistically), but that it doesn't serve

other students (those already inclined to struggle with either Spanish or English academically) by making them basically a-lingual (i.e. non-lingual; no strong language that is definitively theirs).

The dual language is ONE model in the Bilingual Education spectrum. It is a model that only works in SOME classrooms according to the population. I have 22 Spanish speaking kids and I teach ENGLISH math to them. They cannot understand or grasp math concepts because they don't understand the language. If I had a classroom with half of my students being English speakers and half were Spanish speakers, then they would help and support each other. But in a classroom full of Spanish speaking kids, then an early or late exit program would work better.

The first teacher expressed her opinion that the DLBE program only served some students. This belief is not supported by research on DLBE (Collier & Thomas, 2004; Genesee, 1987; Genesee & Lindholm-Leary, 2013; Lindholm-Leary, 2001; Rolstad *et al.*, 2005). Her perspective connected with a relatively common and problematic societal language ideology that students can be 'a-lingual' – a belief that is well refuted in the literature (MacSwan, 2000; Rosa, 2018).

The second teacher articulated a deficit ideology that Spanish-speaking students 'cannot understand or grasp math concepts because they don't understand the language'. For DLBE implementation to be successful, teachers must believe that students are capable of developing and learning in both languages. The teacher continues to explain that she believes the model would work for two-way DLBE, but not work in one-way DLBE, also known as developmental bilingual education, i.e. classrooms that serve all students who are emergent bilingual speakers of Spanish learning English in school. Particularly in a state such as Texas, this is a problematic perception given the number of classrooms with predominantly Spanish speakers.

Investment in DLBE by DLBE teachers in the district

DLBE teachers across the district were asked: How important is dual language implementation to you personally? How important is dual language for your school? How important is dual language for the district? Responses were identified as (a) not important; (b) important; or (c) mixed importance. The teachers were also asked to evaluate their experience with DLBE implementation. These responses were identified as (a) negative; (b) positive; or (c) mixed. Tables 3.3 and 3.4 present the overall findings from these questions across the 20 participants. Given the semi-structured nature of the interviews, not all of the teachers answered

Table 3.3 How important is dual language bilingual education?

	Important	Not important	Mixed importance
Important personally	8 teachers	2 teachers	3 teachers
Important to school	9 teachers	4 teachers	3 teachers
Important to district	6 teachers	3 teachers	5 teachers

Table 3.4 Evaluate your experience with dual language bilingual education

	Positive	Negative	Mixed
Experience with DLBE	5 teachers	8 teachers	7 teachers

each of these questions; this is reflected in the number of teachers in each row of the table.

The majority of the teachers interviewed said that DLBE implementation was important to them, personally. On the other hand, while about half of the participants felt that the dual language program implementation was important to their school, the other half felt that it was not important to their school or they had a mixed opinion about the relative importance of the implementation for the school. The majority of the teachers did not think the implementation was important to the district or they had a mixed opinion about the importance of the implementation for the district.

Teachers articulated more negative statements on the DLBE implementation than positive with respect to the effectiveness of program implementation. However, the majority of statements had a mixed opinion about the effectiveness of program implementation.

In sum, while participants generally viewed the DLBE implementation as important to themselves personally, fewer participants viewed the DLBE implementation as important to their school and the district. Few participants articulated a positive perspective on the effectiveness of the program, while most held a mixed opinion about its effectiveness.

Issues of language policy implementation identified by DLBE teachers

DLBE teachers identified multiple issues of implementation, which can be categorized into three broad themes: (a) investment issues; (b) logistical issues; and (c) structural issues. Each set of issues is presented along with a measure of frequency of occurrence in the data and an illustrative example. The degree of support was defined as the following number of instances: Low = 0–9; Moderate = 10–19; High = 20 and above. A finding that occurred in low frequency was articulated by less than half the participants, while likely all participants articulated a finding that was coded as high frequency.

Investment issues

Table 3.5 presents the issues connected to the investment of the teacher, school or district in the DLBE implementation.

The investment issues were interconnected. It was not surprising that issues of 'fidelity' were brought up in high numbers. Fidelity to the model was often discussed at the district and program level and much of the program and teacher evaluation process was geared toward evaluating 'fidelity' to the model. Teachers' perspectives varied on this issue,

Table 3.5 Investment issues

Issues	Definition	Frequency in interview data	Illustrative example
(1) Fidelity	Comments which refer to teacher or school 'fidelity' or following or not following the model.	High	'En el programa que están ahorita, la misma mierda con diferente nombre si no eres fiel'. [*In the program that they are in right now, it's the same shit with a different name if you are not faithful.*] (Susana, K)
(2) Teacher buy-in	Comments about teacher motivation and buy-in to the program, including teachers discussing personal buy-in or the buy-in of other teachers.	High	'I don't think I embraced implementing it with full fidelity. Sometimes it just doesn't make any sense and it's not effective'. (Daniel, 1st Grade)
(3) Teacher policymaker	Comments in which the teacher is acting as a policymaker. The teacher describes making modifications to the model or making choices for his/her classroom based on his/her beliefs.	High	'I do what I can get away with (laughs)'. (Sandra, pre-K)
(4) DLBE no different	Comments that indicate that the DLBE program is the same as before.	Low	'Para mí es como era la educación bilingüe que ya llevo años haciéndolo y no veo tanta la diferencia'. [*For me it's the same as the bilingual education I have years doing and I don't see much of a difference.*] (Michael, 3rd Grade)

from arguing for a greater need for fidelity, to making comparisons regarding the level of fidelity across classrooms or schools. Fourth-grade teacher Ramón explained how the degree of 'fidelity to the model' varied by teacher, 'El éxito dependería en la manera en que cada uno de los maestros lo implementa (lenguage dual). Hay maestros que sí quieren el programa y hay maestros que no lo quieren, y que al final de cuentas hacen algo totalmente diferente [*Success also depends on the way each teacher implements it (dual language). There are teachers who like the program and others that don't, and in the end, they do things totally different*]'. Mariana (Chapter 5), a third-grade teacher, echoed a similar sentiment, but at the school level: 'Algunas escuelas lo han implementado muy fuertemente y otras de plano lo han quitado. He escuchado de dos o tres escuelas que están siguiendo otro programa en donde solo es inglés [*Some schools are implementing it very strongly and others have simply removed it. I have heard of two or three schools that are following another program where it is English only*]'. Collectively, teachers recognized 'fidelity to the model' as a key issue of implementation at the individual, school and district level.

The issue of fidelity was intimately connected to the issue of teacher investment. There were several teachers whose comments reflected buy-in to the model. Pre-K teacher Marisol (Chapter 4) said, 'A mí me gusta muchísimo el programa dual porque los niños están aprendiendo los dos idiomas y de la misma forma están poniendo la misma importancia en dos idiomas. [*I really like the dual language program because the children are learning the two languages and in the same way they are placing equal importance on the two languages.*]'. However, as demonstrated in the previous section, DLBE implementation was not important to all teachers, which was reflected in additional comments connected to teachers' investment in the model, program implementation and DLBE more broadly. Tamy, a third-grade teacher, was not convinced a single model was appropriate for large-scale implementation. She explained her lack of buy-in stating, 'The decisions that we make should constantly be about what's best for the kids. And if we are more committed to a model than we are to the kids, then it's not going to benefit anyone'. Teachers who were not personally invested in the model often discussed how they adapted the model to the local context. Model adaptations included adjusting the language of instruction (i.e. teaching math in Spanish rather than the model's designated English); changing the interactional components of the model (i.e. not implementing bilingual centers, a key component); and/or changing the physical environment issues of the model (i.e. not having a word wall in both languages, which was a stated requirement in all DLBE classrooms). For example, Irene a pre-K teacher chose to instruct math in Spanish and English. She explained, 'Si yo sigo fielmente el programa dual lenguage, los papás no pueden ayudar en casa porque ellos no saben hablar inglés [*If I follow the dual language program faithfully, parents can't help at home because they do not know how to speak English*]'. Irene felt strongly that her students' success in school was connected to parent support and made a significant model adaptation based on her belief that parents could help more at home if homework was given in Spanish. Given the varying degree of fidelity, teacher buy-in and adaptations to the model, it was also not surprising that a small number of teachers felt that the change in model did not result in any real change at the classroom or school level.

Logistical issues

Another set of issues was connected to the logistics of implementing the DLBE program, depicted in Table 3.6.

Issues of resources fell into two broader categories. First, teachers identified a lack of material resources. This was generally a lack of Spanish materials and curriculum sources. For example, kindergarten teacher Susana said that she made her husband help translate materials at home into Spanish. A second issue was human resources. Teachers brought up both the challenge of finding Spanish teachers as well as Spanish teachers not having high Spanish proficiency levels. Second-grade teacher Chrissy felt that several teachers at her school were not qualified to teach the DLBE program. She identified the first-grade teacher as not being fit, explaining, 'She might have grown up like a little kid speaking Spanish. But she's clearly more comfortable in English'. Several teachers also commented on the difficulty of implementing the 'language of the day' in their school because the administration, teachers and/or the majority of students were English dominant.

Issues of time also fell into two separate categories. Some teachers described the implementation workload as being too demanding. Teachers felt that trying to implement the model took up too much of their time. Edward, a kindergarten teacher, stated, 'Como obstáculo es que demanda trabajo y tiempo para los maestros. [*It demands a lot of work and time for the teachers which is an obstacle.*]'. Other teachers felt that the time allotted to particular activities did not fit the reality of the school schedule. These issues were not connected to teachers feeling that the implementation required too much work, but rather that, logistically, the model was difficult to implement due to daily schedules and routines.

Table 3.6 Logistical issues

Themes	Definition	Frequency in interview data	Illustrative example
(1) Resources	Comments referring to materials or resources needed, (not) provided or desired. This includes human resources including teacher aids or Spanish-speaking staff.	High	'No les han dado las ayudas necesarias para llevar a cabo una clase en los dos idiomas, por ejemplo, la asistencia o los materiales'. [*They have not given the necessary help to carry out a class in two languages, for example, the assistance or the materials.*] (Edward, K)
(2) Time	Comments referring to the amount of time or work that is required by the model, or particular elements of the model.	High	'The number of minutes in it [program model] do not add up to the actual number of minutes that we have in school. They don't take any transition time into consideration at all'. (Maria, pre-K)
(3) Support	Comments addressing the level of support for implementation including the amount of professional development or support from colleagues, administration, training or district.	Moderate	'El apoyo de la escuela que es muy esencial para poder sacarlo adelante'. [*The support from the school is very essential to be able to take it further.*] (Gustavo, 1st Grade)
(4) Prescriptive	Teacher comments needing to follow lots of details, for example word walls in red and blue, or talking about how they have to remember a specific part of the model.	Moderate	'En todas partes (del program) tienes algo para escribir'. [*In all parts (of the program) there is something you have to write.*] (Berta, pre-K)
(5) Mobility	Comments referring to issues with student mobility.	Low	'And, we did start to notice some issues come up with mobility'. (Maria, pre-K)

Teachers feeling that the workload of the program was too demanding, in multiple cases, connected to their perspective that the model was too prescriptive. Participants recognized that the model was complex and had multiple parts. Third-grade teacher Mariana (Chapter 5) explained, 'Siento que tiene más requisitos porque antes teníamos el bilingüe y no era tan requisitoso. [*I feel like it has more requirements because before we had the bilingual and it was not as demanding.*]'. Additional teachers expressed that the prescriptive nature of the model was cumbersome and required too much additional work:

Yo siento que [el programa] es bastante estresante para todos los maestros incluyéndome a mí. Quieren que tengan las palabras, las etiquetas o lo que uno pone [en la paréd], en dos idiomas. Siempre estamos con el estrés que me van a pescar y me van a decir: te falló esto, porque no hay tiempo. [*I feel that it rather stressful for all the teachers including myself. They want you to have the words, the labels, or what someone puts in two languages. We are always with the stress that they are going to catch me, and they are going to tell me: you forgot this, because there is no time.*] (Berta, pre-K)

It's (DLBE program) a lot of environmental print that needs to be up for the kids to see every day and it, it can be overwhelming, because you don't get very many, much wall space and then to be like with the strict obligations and campus obligations. (Deina, 2nd Grade)

It (dual language) created more work for the teachers that were doing it. Um, the district required all of them to have, have two word walls and in certain colors – one was red, one was blue – and so. But and they have to be those colors, not other colors – it had to be those colors. (Jill, pre-K)

Twelve teachers in the sample made comments regarding the prescriptive nature of the model, and, as evidenced, the majority of these teachers held negative views on it. These statements also collectively demonstrated teachers' association of 'dual language' with the specific prescriptive program model. What DLBE means at a theoretical or ideological level (Howard, Lindholm-Leary *et al.*, 2018) differs substantially from an understanding of DLBE as 'the words, the labels, or what someone puts in two languages', 'a lot of environmental print' or 'two word walls and in certain colors'. For several teachers in the sample, their negative view toward the prescriptive model led to the articulation of negative feelings toward DLBE in general.

Student mobility was a final issue brought up in low frequency, and was generally brought up by two-way DLBE teachers. Given that the two-way DLBE programs were contingent on a relatively balanced student population, students entering and exiting the program made it particularly difficult to maintain the balance of students.

Structural issues

Teachers identified issues with DLBE implementation that could not be easily remedied by actions at the individual level; rather, they were structural issues with the implementation. The structural issues identified

Table 3.7 Structural issues

Codes	Definition	Frequency	Illustrative example
Accountability	Comments that address testing or assessment, including teachers talking about test scores or expressing concern about test scores.	High	'They tip their hat to the dual language, but the test wins'. (Samantha, 2nd Grade)
Layered	The mixed messages that teachers receive. Implementation is layered.	High	'La administración, el distrito y el departamento bilingüe, ni ellos están de acuerdo'. [*The administration, district, and bilingual department, not even they are in agreement.*] (Susana, K)
Population	The program is working or not working because of a specific population. The program either does or does not meet the population's needs. Comments that refer to the dual language program working for a specific population of students, a specific grade level or for some students and not others.	High	'Si tienes niños que se portan mal o que tienen problemas de aprendizaje ya todo se te lía y se pierde más tiempo con el sistema de idioma dual'. [*If you have children that behave bad or have learning problems then everything is a mess with dual language system.*] (Edward, K)
Equity	Comments that refer to the model serving one population more than another or comments which refer to an issue of social justice.	Moderate	'I feel like some of the focus has been taken away in the other children that were here first. I guess before the dual language model came along'. (Tamy, 3rd Grade)

arguably represent the most daunting and challenging issues. Table 3.7 presents each issue followed by a discussion of each one in turn.

Accountability

Teachers made statements about the accountability system as a central force of language policy implementation:

All the principals and all the area sups (supervisors) know there is only one thing that they are going to worry about and one thing only. Because if they don't make it (high test scores), they lose their jobs, teachers lose their jobs, and teachers get put on special plans. It is all testing all the time. (Samantha, 2nd Grade)

Al fin al cabo no se manifiesta (dual language) en tercer grado. Es pura teoría porque al fin y al cabo, según los de aquí, lo que necesitamos es ese número de exámen. [*In the end it (dual language) doesn't happen in third grade. It's pure theory because in the end, according to those here, what we need is that number on the exam.*] (Michael, 3rd Grade)

Our area supervisor excludes us from having to do the dual language. Like us in the intermediate grades… We focus on the STAAR. (Deina, 2nd Grade)

In each of these examples, the language policy in the DLBE model was overpowered by the state-mandated accountability system. In the first statement, Samantha indicated that principals and area supervisors (administrator who supervises a group of schools in a region of the city) were not worrying about DLBE policy because they were only worried about testing. Similarly, in the second statement, Michael (Chapter 6) referred to the dual language program and its bilingual language instruction as 'pura teoría [*pure theory*]'. He indexed the administration as 'los de aqui [*those here*]' and emphasized that their priority was the test score. The final statement echoed the same sentiment in which Deina attributed her focus on testing as the direct result of language policy from the area supervisor.

There was a pattern in the responses: comments related to accountability were generally made by higher grade-level teachers. Deina explained, 'I don't think it's the school. I think it's the grade level. I feel like once you get to the third grade, a STAAR (Texas high-stakes standardized testing) grade. They don't, they're not going to push it (DLBE) as much'. Similarly, Daniel, a first-grade teacher, stated, 'I don't see as much enthusiasm from the upper grades'. An inherent tension in the language policy mandates stemmed from high-stakes testing in Texas, which begins in third grade; while the DLBE program promoted bilingual instruction, standardized testing represented *de facto* monolingual language policy (Menken, 2008).

Layered language policy

Given the top-down nature of this policy implementation, the language policy was adopted and renegotiated at the district and school level, reflecting the layered nature of language policy (Hornberger & Johnson, 2007). Teachers had to make their own sense of it for implementation in their classrooms. In the data, 76 statements were coded as *layered*. Teachers made statements interpreting and revoicing (Bakhtin, 1999) what they were supposed to do according to the model, their school or the district's mandates. For example, when Irene (pre-K teacher) was asked what she would do in the scenario in which a student was speaking Spanish during an English class, she responded, 'Según el modelo de Gómez y Gómez, uno debe permitir a los niños hablar el idioma que ellos prefieran [*According to the Gómez y Gómez model, you should allow children to speak in the language they prefer*]'. The use of 'according to' was a frequent linguistic pattern in the data during interviews. In this case, Irene interpreted and revoiced the language policy 'according to the model' when answering a question about her classroom language policy.

In addition to teachers who revoiced a single stakeholder or 'layer', there were teachers who addressed multiple layers directly. The following are three illustrative examples:

> Some of what Gómez and Gómez say go against what the district says and when you ask the question you get a lot of like 'uh, I don't know', and I have two different departments that come to my room with clipboards and grade me on certain things. I work my butt off to make sure I have everything I am supposed to have and then they pick the silliest thing... I guess my issue with Gómez and Gómez is how it's being implemented by the district. (Cathy, K)

> And so, the expectations from the dual language office, versus the expectations from the math office, from the language arts office, are all different, and you don't know who to answer to. And that's, I've said that's the biggest setback – is you don't, you, it is really unclear as to who we are responsible to. (Maria, pre-K)

> We definitely want to do it (dual language). I think parents want it. Administration wants it. Uuum, but I don't know if there is as much communication going on between the classrooms and administration sometimes, and I think administration sometimes feel stuck and can't really do much that they understand where we're coming from, but you know, they have higher-ups, too that they have to respond to. (Daniel, 1st Grade)

In each of the examples, there were conflicts and tension at different layers of policy implementation. In the first statement, Cathy discussed the tension between the demands of the program model, Gómez and Gómez and the district. In the second statement, Maria recognized conflicts between different offices within the district including the dual language, math and language art's offices. Finally, in the third comment, Daniel pointed out that even with participants at different levels (teachers, parents and administration) on board and supporting the program, there is still tension because of miscommunication as well as with 'higher-ups'. Not surprisingly, teachers occasionally expressed frustration or confusion about the mixed messages. Teachers directly stated emotive comments including, I'm 'frustrated' (Daniel), 'mad' (Cathy) and 'overwhelmed' (Deina). Thus, teachers were not only making sense of the language policy, but also the mixed messages from different layers of implementation.

Population

Teachers discussed issues with the implementation based on the local context, particularly the student population. In all cases, the teachers felt that the implementation did not work or was complicated for a particular student group. Teachers identified refugee students, recent immigrants and transfer students as three groups of students. Lucia, a kindergarten teacher, felt that the DLBE implementation was complicated for her school's large refugee population. She pointed out that the refugee students in her classroom spoke more than two languages and commented, 'It (the school) is trying to implement dual language but there are other languages and no helpful resources for them'. Third-grade teacher Michael (Chapter 6) also felt that the model did not properly address newcomers. He felt it was important to use some Spanish during English class for these students even though this would break 'fidelity with the model'. Maria, a pre-K teacher, identified a similar problem with her initially English-dominant-speaking transfer students and explained:

> When I taught second grade dual language, I saw a lot of stress of kids coming in at seven or eight years old that it never spoke Spanish before and then suddenly had to spend half the day doing it. So, unfortunately there are parts of the model we can't implement, because we are playing catch up, because of the mobility.

All three teachers' comments suggested that the diverse linguistic contexts across the district created additional challenges for district-wide DLBE implementation.

Equity

Issues of equity were only brought up in moderate frequency, but the issues identified by the teachers merit additional attention. Student selection for participation in the program; disproportional attention to initially English-dominant speakers; unfair assessment; and inequitable parent reach-out were four issues of equity identified by teachers in the district. Kindergarten teacher Lucia admitted that she was really concerned that the DLBE was 'an enrichment program for wealthy white students', but changed her mind after recognizing that the model was replacing *all* transitional bilingual education programs, which in many cases, served only language-minority students. Indeed, the majority of the equity issues raised by participants were in relation to the two-way DLBE implementation contexts. Third-grade teacher Tamy was particularly concerned with the two-way DLBE implementation at her school. She explained that the combination of neighborhood gentrification with the two-way DLBE implementation resulted in an influx of wealthy white students, which she felt brought 'a whole bunch of new challenges for us as a campus'. She went on to explain:

> There's been a lot of impact that nobody ever anticipated. Just the dichotomy of having so many really poor families and then you got these wealthy families and they have no idea. I think they're not always very understanding. We have some class issues.

Tamy expressed concern about how the increased diversity at her school might create 'an undue burden on the native Spanish speaking kids'. She explained, 'Yes, it's great that the kids (initially English-dominant speakers) are learning to speak Spanish, but if they are learning at the expense of native Spanish speakers, I just think that's not o.k.'. Although Tamy felt that the DLBE implementation brought unanticipated challenges, she expressed hope for moving forward. She explained that her school principal was very supportive of teacher decision-making including model adaptations.

Tamy was not the only teacher to identify issues of equity with the model implementation. Pre-K teacher Jill explained that at her school the 'white kids go to dual language' while the African American students do not. Jill explained that the segregation happening at her school was a major problem: 'What we're doing here, it's not equitable'. Inequities in DLBE program implementation have been identified in prior research (Cervantes-Soon, 2014; López & Fránquiz, 2009). Ongoing research exploring these issues of equity is critical for the advancement of DLBE.

Implications of District-Wide Findings for Case Studies

It is clear that as researchers we need a more complex understanding of the processes that educators are required to undertake in the midst of implementing DLBE programs. If we are to offer practical and theoretically grounded advice for educators committed to implementing additive programs and improving the educational experiences of EBs, we need to better understand what educators are facing. This synthesis of teacher perspectives is a barebones beginning. We hope that the case studies in the chapters that follow will flesh out the picture a bit more, but we acknowledge the impossibility of fully capturing this phenomenon. We merely provide some thought-provoking slices of the experience in the hopes of engaging educators and researchers in productive ongoing discussion. The majority of the issues identified through the thematic analysis are established in the literature and common to educational implementation in general (Calderón & Minaya-Rowe, 2003; Freeman, 2004; Howard & Sugarman, 2007; Lindholm-Leary, 2001, 2005; Pérez, 2004). That said, it is important to consider how these issues appear connected to or potentially exacerbated by the top-down, large-scale nature of this initiative.

One such issue was teachers' perception of the level of investment of their school or district in the implementation. While most teachers stated that the DLBE implementation was important to them, fewer teachers expressed that the DLBE implementation was important for their school or district. For a large-scale implementation starting at the district level, district officials must first ensure buy-in from participating school leaders including principals. One suggestion might be to begin with professional development on DLBE theory at the administrative and educational leader level.

This chapter highlighted the layered nature of policy implementation from a teachers' perspective. Administrators have to be particularly careful in a top-down model to directly address layering. District and school leaders must recognize how the DLBE initiative will work alongside additional district or school initiatives to prevent sending mixed messages to teachers. This created both confusion and frustration among teachers.

According to teachers, a major competing force with the DLBE implementation was standardized testing. If accountability for assessment (another top-down initiative) drowns out or overwhelms accountability for DLBE implementation, the program effectiveness will likely suffer, which is an important finding for leaders. Direct instruction and discussion about expectations for DLBE implementation and standardized assessment are required. Ironically, the district adopted the DLBE program in part to improve standardized test scores, and yet the pressure for short-term success on these monolingual exams contributed to the lack of teacher and administrator buy-in. Previous research demonstrates that the additive goals of DLBE, bilingualism, biculturalism and biliteracy can conflict with accountability pressure to perform well on monolingual exams (Menken, 2008; Pérez, 2004). Again, ongoing professional development about the educational theory behind DLBE seems critical if we want to address issues of buy-in and the long-term benefits of bilingualism and bilingual education for EBs.

While this district's adopted language policy was highly prescriptive, teachers still adapted the policy to fit the needs of their students or reflect their own ideologies and beliefs (Hornberger & Johnson; 2007; Menken & García, 2010). Teachers faced unique challenges and opportunities based on the local context including the student population. A top-down implementation should recognize the need for local adaptation and should incorporate flexibility for change into the model. One suggestion is for the top-down process to also include an organizational learning process in which policies from the top are adjusted based on teachers' experiences. In other words, local interpretations and adaptations can be viewed as a type of organizational learning in which the leadership must adapt the top-down strategies/policies to accommodate the teachers' ideas that result from local interpretation. This, of course, would require leaders who listen, leaders who are not just politically motivated.

Large-scale DLBE implementation is an opportunity to provide additive bilingual education to large numbers of EBs. However, this chapter highlighted several of the challenges with a top-down approach from teachers' perspectives based on their implementation experiences. We need to listen to teachers and value their professional insights based on experience in order for these top-down implementation efforts to make meaningful improvements in students' bilingual education.

In the following three chapters, you will meet six teachers who participated in the DLBE implementation process. As you read, please consider the following questions:

- How do the teacher's own ideologies about language and bilingualism impact their classroom?
- How does the teacher's identity (race, ethnicity, language background, teaching experiences, etc.) appear to impact the classroom interactions?
- How do district policies help and hinder the teacher's efforts to serve their students?

The case studies are organized to facilitate the synthesis of these questions and others. In each chapter, when we introduce a teacher, we include information about the teacher's background, followed by a description of the teacher's classroom language policy that begins with a vignette based on observations. We include the vignette in order to give the reader a glimpse into the classroom.

As described previously, the following three chapters are grouped thematically, starting with teachers who attempted to implement the model with fidelity (Chapter 4), followed by teachers who struggled to implement the model (Chapter 5) and ending with teachers who adapted the model during implementation (Chapter 6). Yet, as we have also already mentioned, the issues in the chapters overlap and, at times, the findings are not consistent, and even contradictory. As such, each chapter also tackles one of the key tensions that surfaced in the data discussed in the final section.

4 Teacher Cases: Implementing DLBE with Fidelity or Language Separation in a Bilingual Context

School districts and schools attempting to implement dual language bilingual education (DLBE) are sure to hear about the importance of *fidelity to the model* or the degree to which the delivery of the program adheres to the model design. Chapter 3 demonstrated how *fidelity to the model* was an issue of implementation articulated by teachers across the district. Teacher perspectives varied on this issue, from arguing for the need for higher fidelity to expressing the desire for more flexibility within the model. But everybody appeared to agree that the DLBE implementation was being done with different degrees of fidelity to the model across schools and within schools across classrooms. This chapter goes into more depth on this issue, presenting the cases of two teachers who were committed to implementing the model with fidelity.

Multiple scholars in DLBE research acknowledge the critical role of consistency and adherence to program design. Thomas and Collier are two often-cited scholars who provide professional development nationally on the topic (www.thomasandcollier.com). In their research, they identify essential elements to successful DLBE implementation, one of which is the program design (Collier & Thomas, 2004). One consistent characteristic of DLBE program models is the separation of language for instruction. As mentioned, the Gómez and Gómez Dual Language Enrichment model divided language of instruction by content area, and program implementation stressed fidelity to the model (Dual Language Training Institute, 2018). However, a new vein of research has emerged questioning the strict separation of language in DLBE (García, 2009a; Palmer, Martínez *et al.*, 2014). Furthermore, bilinguals in Texas naturally intermingle their language practices – especially those who were raised bilingually (Sayer, 2013). Given that most DLBE models are designed based on strict separation of language, this creates a tension for teachers who may themselves regularly engage their full linguistic repertoire across all their languages, but who are being asked to demonstrate fidelity to the model that requires them to engage only one 'named language' in any given lesson. In Chapter 6, we examine two teachers who adapted and changed the model to incorporate more linguistic flexibility and hybridity in the classroom.

This chapter considers two teachers, Marisol and Rachel, who articulated strong support for the program and embodied fidelity to the model in their classrooms. The discussion will consider the teachers' commitment to implementing the model with fidelity and the mediating factors including their language ideologies and professional identities. Marisol and Rachel's two cases collectively demonstrate how fidelity to the model and teachers' efforts to strictly separate languages during academic instruction in some ways resulted in protected spaces for language development, yet potentially limited spaces for bilingual language development in other ways. We discuss this central tension and implications for DLBE implementation at the end of the chapter.

Marisol: Pre-K One-Way DLBE Teacher

Background

Marisol was a pre-K teacher with nine years of teaching experience in two districts. She worked for six years in third grade at the first district. She had been in the second district at the Village Pre-Kindergarten School (pseudonym) for three years at the time of data collection. Of her nine years of teaching experience, six were in a DLBE program. Marisol self-identified as Latina, female and bilingual. She grew up in Texas near the border with Mexico and her home language was Spanish. Her education was in English-only, which she described as a difficult and, at times, painful experience. She attributed her passion and dedication to bilingual education to her personal negative educational experiences and expressed the desire to prevent her students from experiencing what she went through in school. This connected to her dedication to work in schools that served low-income Latinx families: 'I want to work in a low-income community just because I feel for them. I know what they are going through'. Marisol described her dedication to working at the Village Pre-Kindergarten; she commuted an hour and a half daily to work with this particular community of students and turned down an offer to work at a predominantly white school closer to her home.

At the time of the study, the Village Pre-Kindergarten School, a state-funded pre-kindergarten, was approximately 89% Hispanic, 97%

economically disadvantaged and 71% English language learners (ELLs). Students qualified to attend the school based on language-minority status or low socioeconomic level. The Village Pre-Kindergarten School was implementing one-way (OW) DLBE programs (all of the students in the classroom were ELLs) alongside general education classrooms.

Marisol worked in a self-contained pre-K classroom. She had 17 students: 9 boys and 8 girls. She described her students' linguistic proficiencies and said, 'Todos están en diferentes niveles. Miro que algunos tienen inglés mucho más que otros y hay unos que no han estado expuestos al inglés, hay una variedad en el nivel que está [*They are all at different level. I see that some have much more English than others that have not been exposed to English. There is variation in the level that they are at*]'. Her description reflected an awareness of variation in linguistic development and the bilingual continua, specifically the simultaneous/sequential continua that distinguish between children exposed to bilingual practices from a young age versus at an older age, often with the start of formal schooling (Fitts, 2006; Hornberger, 2002). When asked if all of the students spoke Spanish, she responded:

> Sí, la mayoría habla español, ¿a qué nivel? Depende, tengo un niño que usa spanglish, unos que hacen code-switching, y hay otros que nada más solo español y cada vez que hacemos inglés comienzan a llorar porque no les gusta el inglés. [*Yes, the majority speak Spanish. At what level? It depends, I have a boy who uses Spanglish, some who do code-switching, and there are others who only use Spanish and every time we do English they begin to cry because they don't like English.*]

In this statement, Marisol separated Spanish, code-switching and Spanglish into distinct categories. Marisol articulated her perspective of Spanglish in an interview:

> Lo entiendo, pero no creo que es apropiado. Deberíamos de captar un idioma, tener una buena fundación y después agarrar el otro y así agarrar los dos. Pero tener los dos muy bien porque suena feo cuando uno está hablando... para mí no los consideraría tan inteligentes como otras personas porque pienso que lo están revolviendo. [*I understand it, but I don't think it is appropriate. We should gain one language, have a good foundation and afterward pick up another one and in that way pick up both. But you should have both really well or it sounds ugly when someone is speaking... I don't consider them as intelligent as other people because I think they are mixing it up.*]

This quote demonstrates Marisol's articulated perspective that 'non-standard' language was not 'appropriate' and that Spanglish 'sounds ugly', reflecting a dominant societal ideology of linguistic purism. She believed that sequential bilingualism (learning one language before learning the second) was superior to simultaneous bilingual development. Her orientation reflected 'dual monolingualism' (Fitts, 2006) where bilinguals are viewed as two monolinguals in one. Marisol's embodied classroom practices did not always align with her articulated negative perspective on Spanglish. The next section explores Marisol's classroom language policy including the teacher and students' language practices.

Classroom language policy

Students sing out numbers in English to the 'Number Rock' video on YouTube projected on the whiteboard. Some students sing along the entire time to the rote counting and repetition. Other students shout out certain numbers 'one, two' but just dance as the numbers get higher. The teacher approaches Marco who is dancing around his classmate, 'You know what dancing in place is mijo [my son]? Dancing in place means I don't leave my place'. The teacher takes out a large plastic microphone and hands it to Alexa, who sings into the microphone, 'one, two' before passing it to her classmate Nico who continues, 'three, four'. There is a palpable feeling of student energy and controlled chaos vibrating through the room.

As the 'Number Rock' song comes to an end, Marisol directs students in English to stop dancing and singing and to sit in their designated spots on the carpet. Marco says out loud, 'Si, en la carpeta [yes, on the carpet]'. As the students settle down, the teacher sits down in the circle and calls for attention in English. The teacher redirects in English several times before all students are sitting quietly. Once she has all students' attention, Marisol explains, 'We are going to continue working on addition. Addition means putting together things'. She calls on a student, Lucia, to explain addition. Lucia explains in Spanish, 'Es cuando te pones una cosa con otra cosa'. Marisol praises Lucia, 'Very good!' before introducing the English book, 'Today we are going to read Dora's eggs. We are going to work on our counting and addition as we read it together'. Marisol begins to read the book. She pauses on different pages and asks students questions, 'How many piglets are there?' Students answer in both Spanish and English. Diego asks a question in Spanish. Marisol ignores him. Mariela asks a question in English and Marisol responds. When the teacher finishes the book, she tells students it is time for math centers with their bilingual pair. She releases students two by two based on who is sitting quietly and paying attention.

A little later: Marisol checks her stopwatch. Math center time is coming to an end, and she prepares to transition to science. She places the English math book 'Dora's eggs' aside and pulls out the Spanish book 'Pollito Chiquito'. She rings the bell indicating to her students that center time is over. One by one students put away their centers activity and take a seat on the carpet. '¡Te estamos esperando Marco [We are waiting on you Marco]!' shouts Marisol as students are settling on the carpet. Marisol continues, 'Esta semana en ciencias, vamos a aprender sobre un montón de animales y los sonidos que hacen. [This week in science, we are going to learn about a ton of animals and the sounds they make.]' A few students clap. Diego shouts out, '¡Ya sé! [I already know!]' Marco shouts, 'Yes!' Marisol continues the lesson in Spanish with her students' full attention and excitement to learn about ovejas [sheep], vacas [cows] and el pollito chiquito [the little chick].

Marisol followed the district's DLBE language policy with high fidelity in her classroom. Math was taught in English. During all classroom observations and video-recordings of math instruction ($n = 8$), only one discrepant case was included in the vignette in which she spoke Spanish to say 'mijo [*my son*]', which is a common term of endearment in Spanish. Science, social studies and language arts were taught in Spanish. During all classroom observations and video-recordings of language arts and science instruction ($n = 6$), she was only observed saying 'okay' in English; all else was in Spanish. The language used during transition times was based on the language of the day. During transition times ($n = 15$), she was observed adhering to the language policy and speaking Spanish on Spanish days (M/W/F) and English on English days (T/TH).

The way Marisol discussed her classroom language policy very much aligned with what we observed of her classroom practices. Marisol supported the DLBE program and articulated that she felt the problem with implementation was teachers' not adhering to the model. In fact, Marisol disproportionately responded to students during English instruction when the students engaged in English. This was illustrated in the vignette in the way Marisol ignored Diego's Spanish response, but responded to Mariela's English comment. However, this was not always the case. Because students predominantly engaged in Spanish, Marisol was also observed responding in English to student comments in Spanish – a practice that is quite acceptable within the dictates of the DLBE model at the pre-kindergarten level. Regardless of student language choice, however, Marisol always responded in English, maintaining language separation and fidelity to the model.

Students were observed engaging in different language practices in Marisol's classroom. Given the age (pre-K) and context (OW DLBE), it was not surprising that students predominantly engaged in Spanish. However, as demonstrated in the vignette, students engaged in English practices during the designated English time, particularly during direct instruction and carpet time.

Students' fluid language practices including Spanish, Spanglish and linguistic shifting were also present in every observation in Marisol's classroom. For example, in the vignette, Marco said 'sí, en la carpeta'. Carpeta is a Spanish to English loanword, emerging from the English 'carpet', associated with Spanglish (the standard Mexican Spanish word 'carpeta' refers to a folder or notebook). Over the course of observations, Marisol was never observed or video-recorded 'correcting' or repairing students' language practices, specifically students shifting language practices or the use of non-standard Spanish. She also displayed no reaction to a loudspeaker announcement that included Spanglish. The announcement was given three times, asking someone to move their 'troca azul [*blue truck*]'. Similar to 'carpeta (*carpet*)', 'troca' is an English loanword identified as Spanglish. This ideological embodiment (not reacting to or correcting Spanglish) did not necessarily align with her articulated perspective.

Teacher repair of student language practices is a form of language ideology in practice (Razfar, 2005). Marisol's absence of student redirection fits with the Gómez and Gómez model's language policy wherein teachers are encouraged to strictly separate their language, but to be more accepting of a variety of student language practices (Dual Language Training Institute, 2018). The observations afford nuance into understanding Marisol's language ideologies. While she articulated a negative perspective toward non-standard language practice, she did not embody this language ideology in her local classroom language policy. She did not correct students and she had no reaction to the use of Spanglish over the loudspeaker.

An informal retrospective interview with Marisol offered additional complexity to our understanding of her language ideologies, and how they were embodied in her classroom language policy and practices:

Katy: What do you think of the use of Spanglish over the loudspeaker?

Marisol: Not good, but at the same time I know that a lot of them don't have Spanish and I can't criticize because I am not anywhere near there either.

Katy: [in terms] of Spanish proficiency?

Marisol: Uh huh. At least I don't feel adequate.
Katy: You feel stronger in English?
Marisol: Unfortunately, in neither.

When Marisol commented 'a lot of them don't have Spanish', she implied that someone who uses Spanglish does not 'have' Spanish. Marisol articulated the notion that someone could 'not have' a language, representing a societal ideology of languagelessness (Rosa, 2018). One can only claim a language, it seems, if one speaks a 'standard' register.

Then Marisol reflected on her own language practices, saying that she did not 'feel adequate'. She believed she was not strong in Spanish or English. This appeared to represent an internalization of dominant or standard language ideologies, a form of linguistic oppression. Marisol was a bilingual educator with years of experience who adeptly and easily shifted between languages for content instruction in both English and Spanish. The power of this dominant societal language ideology resulted in a trained and experienced bilingual teacher articulating linguistic insecurity. Marisol's experiences with linguistic supremacy, including her English-only childhood schooling experience, connected to her complex articulated and embodied language ideologies. She was aware of social justice issues involving her students' identities as Latinxs but appeared less in tune with how the processes of marginalization manifested through standard language ideologies.

Dominant language ideologies influenced Marisol's instruction in other ways, such as her daily frustration with one of her students, Marco. As demonstrated in the vignette, Marco was frequently redirected and engaged in Spanglish. When asked about Marco, she described him as 'low in both languages'. She explained her perspective saying, 'I think he's mixing both of them up. They [His parents] definitely are not doing what I've asked them to do, which is concentrate on one [language]. That is my theory'. In advising Marco's parents to modulate their (bilingual) home language practices, it appeared that Marisol was drawing on an internalized language ideology that labeled hybrid language practices as semi- or alingual (MacSwan, 2000). In fact, Marisol recommended placing Marco in an English-medium classroom for the following year, essentially ending his bilingual schooling experiences in kindergarten.

Marisol's dedication to improving the schooling experiences of her Spanish-speaking students made her an advocate of DLBE and influenced her classroom behaviors and decisions to implement the model with fidelity. There were protected spaces for English and Spanish development, and students were observed engaging in these distinct language practices during these designated times. Bilingual development was taking place in her classroom in meaningful and intentional ways. Yet, Marisol's own language ideologies, particularly her beliefs about language acquisition and the importance of language separation, represented and reinforced by the model, resulted in her not viewing DLBE as a space appropriate for all children. In the case of Marco, she decided that a simultaneous bilingual child whose first language could best be described as Spanglish would be more successful in a generalist classroom with only one language. As a result, a bilingual child was denied access to a bilingual education and the opportunity to continue to develop his biliteracy.

Rachel: Third-Grade Two-Way DLBE Co-Teacher (English Side)

Background

Rachel identified as a white female in her late twenties. This was her first year at Woodward Elementary; however, she had two years of experience teaching second grade in a non-bilingual classroom at a different school in the district. Rachel had received her certification through a popular local alternative certification program. Having majored in Spanish in college and having spent two years in Madrid, she identified as bilingual in Spanish and English. Given that Rachel learned Spanish as an adult and in a foreign language context, her individual bilingual language development trajectory was distinct from the students in her classroom. Rachel could best be described as a sequential bilingual (having learned her second language sequentially after her first), while many of Rachel's students were simultaneous bilinguals (having learned both Spanish and English from birth). Rachel intentionally sought out and applied to teach in a two-way (TW) DLBE program and was thrilled to have the opportunity to work at Woodward Elementary.

Woodward Elementary was a medium-sized urban school situated within a largely Hispanic community. At the time of the study, the school was approximately 87% Hispanic, 97% eligible for free or reduced-price lunch and 75% 'limited English proficient'. Woodward was 1 of 10 pilot schools in the district implementing a DLBE program model. Woodward elected to implement both the OW and TW DLBE program. For example, in third grade, they had a OW DLBE classroom made up entirely of students labeled ELLs and taught by a self-contained teacher; two TW DLBE classrooms that served both ELLs and initially English-dominant speakers co-taught by two teachers, with Rachel delivering the English-medium part of the curriculum; and one mainstream classroom taught by an English as a second language (ESL)-certified teacher.

Rachel co-taught two groups of children for the TW DLBE program with her co-teacher Lisel (Chapter 5). Despite the TW DLBE program label, there were very few initially English-dominant speakers. In Rachel's homeroom, there was one initially English-dominant speaker and in Lisel's homeroom, there were four; however, the labels were insufficient to capture the complex linguistic repertoires of the students. Research suggests that language dominance is not fixed (Genesee, 2001) and can shift based on motivation, preference or situation (Meisel, 2007). Indeed, every student in the classroom was better conceptualized as being on different points along the bilingual/biliterate continua (Hornberger, 2003). While only five students were labeled 'native English speakers', eight students were identified as stronger in English and designated to take their standardized tests in English for reading. The classroom demographics mirrored the demographics of the school; almost all of the students were Latina/o and came from low-socioeconomic status households.

Rachel articulated being disappointed by the lack of initially English-dominant speakers in her two classes:

> It was a sad day when I got my class list. … I … changed schools because of the two-way dual, and then yeah of the forty kids there's four English speakers and so I don't know why those kids have left. I don't know if it has to do with the school or if it is just demographics. I wish that I had been better informed about it before I took the position. (Ms Reese, 10/2012)

The principal confirmed in an interview that, indeed, many of the initially English-dominant-speaking students had withdrawn by the end of second grade, partly because their middle-class white parents opted to move them to schools with less focus on testing (see Chapter 5). Given that Rachel had purposefully switched schools to participate in the TW DLBE program, she had expected more cultural and linguistic diversity. And yet, Rachel described her students' language practices in additive ways as strong in both English and Spanish. In all our interactions with her, she never articulated a negative perspective about her students' language abilities or practices including any engagement in hybrid or non-standard practices. However, as the following section illustrates, students really only engaged with Rachel in English. When Rachel was asked by her principal what language different students would take their state test in (a common discussion point in Texas elementary schools in third through fifth grades), Rachel strongly expressed that all of her students could and should be tested in English, and they did. As will be shown in

Chapter 5, this important language policy decision had implications for her students and for the TW DLBE program. The following snapshot illustrates Rachel's classroom language policy and how all the students were instructed, prepared and ultimately assessed in English.

Classroom language policy

After finishing a mini-lecture on fractions entirely in English, Rachel directed her students, 'We are going to work on some fraction math problems. Please get with your bilingual partner'. Rachel delivered the instructions orally enunciating every syllable and also provided the instructions visually in writing on the PowerPoint. Students transitioned quickly to turning and talking with their partner and working through the math problems. They knew exactly what they were supposed to be doing; pair work was a common routine with clear expectations. Rachel began to walk around and monitor the room. She walked up to Ana and Monica and asked, 'How are you doing? Do you have any questions?' Ana responded to the teacher, 'No, we are good'. Ana points to the math problem in front of her and turns to her partner Monica and asks, 'What do you think this number is?' Rachel walks away to another table. Once Rachel is out of earshot, Monica asks Ana, 'A ver, ¿cuál? [Wait, which one?]' Ana responds, 'This one (pointing at the top number on the fraction), lo de arriba [the one on top]'.

Rachel continues to walk and monitor students around the room. She gets to a pair of students, Gerardo and Victoria, that are struggling with a problem and asks them to come to the U-shaped table in the corner of the room. Rachel sits in the center of the U across from the two students and begins to scaffold, 'Gerardo, point to the numerator. (Gerardo points). And, Victoria if that is the numerator, which is the number on the bottom?' Victoria responds, 'The denominator'. Rachel continues on with Gerardo and Victoria step by step. Rachel, Gerardo and Victoria engage in English only. The other students are working with their partners, drawing freely on their full linguistic repertoires to solve the problems including Spanish, English and a mixture of the two. No teacher redirection is observed. Students know what to do and have adeptly learned how to linguistically navigate the different classroom spaces.

Just like Marisol, Rachel followed the district DLBE language policy with high fidelity. As the official 'English side' teacher in the TW program, Rachel was supposed to teach her subjects (math and language arts) only in English. Rachel's language practices were consistent; Rachel was only observed speaking English to her students despite her bilingual capability. She implemented a number of scaffolding strategies for comprehensible input. Students were only observed speaking English to Rachel, except for one case in which a student said *sí* instead of 'yes'. Katy even noted in her field notes after her first classroom observation: *As of now, I have heard students speaking Spanish to each other but not to the teacher.* This pattern was remarkably consistent across all the observations as well as analysis of audio and video recordings.

As illustrated in the vignette, over time, we realized that students appeared to speak more in English with teacher proximity. Students appeared to modify their language choices based not only on whom they were talking to, but also on the proximity of the teacher. The pattern of students speaking only English when the teacher was near was generally consistent, yet there were two noted instances during observations in which the pattern broke. In the following example, the teacher was sitting at a table in the corner of the room used to meet with individual students, pairs or groups. Rachel announced to students that she would be calling a group to work with her. She called five student names. Mariela was one of the students, and Rachel asked Mariela if Leslie was in the bathroom.

> **Mariela:** (*facing and talking to teacher*) No, she is at the computer. (*turns about 45 degrees in the direction of Leslie*) Leslie, *te habla la maestra* [Leslie, the teacher is calling you].

The specific reason for Mariela's switch into Spanish is difficult to pinpoint given the dominant language pattern in the classroom to only speak English with teacher proximity. It is possible Mariela typically interacted with Leslie in Spanish. Perhaps she was distancing herself from the teacher and demonstrating solidarity and camaraderie with her classmate. An alternative explanation was that the phrase '*te habla la maestra*' was formulaic speech repeated frequently within classroom discourse. Or, Mariela's shift was perhaps simply an illustration of the local hybrid language practices of her community; shifting language practices between interlocutors was a daily phenomenon in this linguistically diverse community in other classroom and school spaces.

In addition to Mariela's noticeable break from the overall pattern of students speaking only English with teacher proximity, during a whole-class observation, two boys at different tables in the classroom shouted out Spanish comments across the room. Given that their shouts were loud enough for everyone to hear, this instance also broke with the pattern. Rachel was walking the students through a poetry lesson; she had the students close their eyes and imagine what they could see from the poem's descriptive language. Several boys did not close their eyes, which caused them to discreetly giggle and make subtle glances toward one another. When the students were asked to open their eyes and share something they saw, one boy said, 'I saw a shadow'. The teacher praised and repeated his answer and told everyone to write down what they had seen. As students began to write, the teacher walked toward the table closest to the wall, distancing her from the boys who were giggling, and began to monitor student work. A space opened up for the boys to communicate with each other:

1   **Boy1** (loud enough for boys at three different tables to hear him): *Yo estaba así* [I was like this]. *Yo estaba así* [I was like this] (glancing at the different boys at the table and modeling with his hands how he had made it look like he was covering his eyes while in reality maintaining vision)
2   **Boy2** (shouting): *Yo miré* shadow [I saw shadow]
3   Several boys (rocking back and forth laughing)

Although the second boy's gesture was not observed when he made the comment, we inferred that he was covering his eyes and still looking and commenting on how he could literally see a shadow from his hand. In this event, the students still seemed aware of teacher proximity – it mediated when they shouted to one another. They waited until the teacher was across the room. However, the shouting was loud enough for the teacher to also hear it. Thus, as with Mariela's comment, this was a discrepant case.

This language event revealed some potentially interesting uses of Spanish or shifting language practices in the classroom as a form of student agency. It appeared as though the boys were shouting to each other in Spanish as a covert way to discuss their local act of resistance, in this case, not shutting their eyes. Their Spanish language use with one another positioned them socially distant from the English-speaking teacher. The student who said, '*Yo miré* shadow' was drawing on the word *shadow* from the poetry lesson but repurposing its meaning; the 'shadow' image in the poem versus the 'shadow' created by his hands. His election to use the Spanish 'yo mire' was potentially a subtle and creative way to indicate this change in meaning of the word *shadow* and its potential underlying purpose of student resistance.

In an informal retrospective interview with Rachel, Katy discussed her observations of classroom language practices. She told Rachel she observed her only speaking in English and the students only speaking to her in English. Rachel confirmed both to be true. Then, Katy shared her observation that the students do speak in Spanish and mix language practices with each other. In reaction, Rachel gave a surprised look (eyebrows lifted) and said, 'They should only be speaking in English'. She appeared to be expressing both disbelief and concern, commenting that she had only noticed students speaking Spanish when they were 'misbehaving or off-task'.

Her surprise – and discomfort – surprised us; we were under the assumption that Rachel supported her students' use of Spanish with each other, given the prominence of Spanish and the shifting of language practices in student interactions throughout our observation times in the classroom. Our observation that students were speaking more English the closer they were to the teacher became more meaningful; it appeared that students had found the 'wiggle room' and were enacting their agency to engage in their community hybrid language practices when the teacher was at a distance (Erickson, 2004). Rachel's reaction also shed a new light on our interpretation of the boys shouting to each other in Spanish across the room. Indeed, the students seemed to be designating Spanish and hybridity, in part, as a space for resistance. The overall frequent use of Spanish and the shifting of language practices within peer interactions likely reflected that the practices were natural and spontaneous (Reyes, 2001). The students were drawing on their linguistic repertoires, including their bilingual competencies. In other words, in these peer interactions, students continued to be bilingual regardless of what the 'official' model and classroom policy dictated.

Rachel's strict separation of language resulted in students engaging in and developing their English language practices. Rachel had clear and high expectations with her classroom language policy. Students regulated their language practices and engaged only in English when she was nearby. Rachel's confidence in her students' English language abilities was demonstrated through her decision that all students should take the standardized math exam in English. At the same time, her students found spaces to draw on their full linguistic repertoire for meaning-making and problem-solving. Rachel's perception that her students only used Spanish when they were 'misbehaving or off-task' was not consistent with our observations: students were using Spanish when collaborating with one another in their bilingual pairs on math problems, for instance. We wondered what additional possibilities for meaning-making would have been practicable if Rachel had been more aware of her students' Spanish use and capitalized on their full linguistic repertoires in intentional and strategic ways for accessing content.

Discussion

Fidelity to the DLBE model, teacher buy-in and ideological alignment

Marisol and Rachel both implemented the model with fidelity in large part based on their larger commitment to bilingual education and to DLBE specifically. As such, the DLBE model mediated the classroom language policy including the spaces for different language practices. The model divided language of instruction by content area, and correspondingly, Marisol and Rachel taught their subjects according to the designated language, for example, both taught math entirely in English. Their investment in DLBE was connected to their personal teaching and schooling experiences. Having attended school with English-only instruction as a child, Marisol wanted to provide her students with a different schooling experience that valued bilingualism. She was passionate about the broader aims and goals of bilingual education, particularly an approach that placed equal value on both languages. Rachel changed schools specifically in order to participate in the TW DLBE program. She positioned herself as an expert on the model multiple times and understood her role as the English teacher to speak English only. In sum, both teachers were invested in the model to a high degree.

Marisol and Rachel were also aligned ideologically with the model's policy of strict language separation. As we explore in Chapter 6, not all teachers prescribed to this language policy. Again, these ideologies were connected to their own schooling and teaching experience. Marisol articulated her belief that language acquisition was most successful when there was a strong base in one language before attempting to learn or add on a second. She perceived hybrid language practices and Spanglish as a problem. In fact, Marisol perceived her own bilingualism as 'not adequate' because she herself engaged in these practices. Her own experience with linguistic oppression likely connected to the internalization of this dominant societal ideology. This could possibly explain the inconsistency between her articulated and embodied language ideologies – her stated belief that engaging in hybrid language practices was wrong while she never actually corrected these practices when they occurred around her. Rachel, on the other hand, was a sequential bilingual. She learned English first, followed by Spanish later in school. A policy of strict separation of languages was consistent with her own language learning experience. Interestingly, her alignment of articulated and embodied ideologies was powerful. Rachel both articulated and embodied an English-only ideology, and consistently students treated her as an English-only interlocutor (while continuing to embody bilingualism when they caught some distance from her). Ironically, Rachel's 'English-only' ideology was for the purpose of bilingual development; she was upholding her half of the model.

Tension: Strict separation of languages vs bilingual practices and identities

Both Marisol and Rachel implemented the model with a high degree of fidelity. When Marisol switched content areas (i.e. going from math to science), she intentionally and noticeably switched languages to align with the designated language of instruction. Rachel, who was assigned to implement the English portion of the curriculum, adhered strictly to English despite her self-identification as bilingual. Marisol and Rachel were enacting professional identities that followed the top-down language policy mandate. For school and district administrators tasked with implementing a program, teachers such as Marisol and Rachel make their lives easier. Both teachers created protected spaces for language development and expertly fulfilled their teaching duties.

And yet, in both cases, this strict separation of language did not mirror the language ecology of the classroom, specifically the student language practices. The embedded message that bilingualism needs to be hidden – or that in order to develop bilingualism students need to engage monolingually – seems to contradict the additive goals of bilingualism and biliteracy in DLBE. As such, in both classrooms, the policy of strict language separation created some problematic tension. Marisol positioned her student Marco, who engaged the most in Spanglish, as not fit for bilingual education. Marisol perceived Marco as confused and 'low in both languages' because he failed to engage consistently in language practices identified as Spanish or English. In truth, the bilingual education model did not fit him as it did not value, allow or create spaces for him to use his full linguistic repertoire as a resource (García, 2009a). In Rachel's classroom, students expertly hid their bilingual language practices. We observed students on-task using their Spanish for meaning-making, and yet, they had to be covert. Publicly, Spanish and hybridity became the classroom language of resistance, or as Rachel noted, the language for 'misbehaving'. Rather than celebrate and foster bilingual identities and bilingual practices, the message was that monolingual, standardized practices are the target.

We will return to a discussion and consideration of the ways translanguaging can be utilized as a resource for students' academic, social and bilingual identity development in Chapter 6 when we present two teachers who adapted the model to their local context. First, in Chapter 5, we meet two teachers who struggled to implement the model despite their quite clear investment and ideological alignment with the program initiative.

Discussion Questions

(1) In what ways did Marisol and Rachel's identities and experiences connect to their classroom language practices?
(2) Reflect on your own beliefs about language as well as your own language practices and language learning experiences. How and in what ways are they connected?

5 Teacher Cases: Struggling to Implement DLBE or Multiple and Contradictory Policy Mandates

In a large-scale educational initiative, it is common for there to be obstacles, challenges and ultimately variation in the degree of successful implementation. As reviewed in Chapter 2, successful implementation of dual language bilingual education (DLBE) programs requires more than fulfilling the practical programmatic needs (Calderón & Minaya-Rowe, 2003; Cloud *et al.*, 2000; Howard & Sugarman, 2007; Lindholm-Leary, 2001, 2005). Effective DLBE implementation requires effective leadership, a conducive school environment, empowerment and respect for students and a supportive school culture (Howard & Sugarman, 2007; Lindholm-Leary, 2001). In our district-wide research (see Chapter 3), we learned that, according to educators, among the issues of implementation occurring across the district were access to materials, minimal professional development and lack of training. In particular, mandates related to high-stakes standardized testing conflicted with DLBE implementation. This chapter takes a closer look at the struggles faced by two third-grade teachers in their classrooms. In Texas, third and fifth grade are notorious for being high pressure for teachers based on the high-stakes testing that occurs at these grade levels. These case studies illustrate how teachers are burdened with juggling multiple, and sometimes contradictory, language policy demands. The closing discussion will focus on the central tension for educators trying to prepare students for a monolingual standardized assessment alongside trying to implement an educational program with the goals of bilingualism and biliteracy.

Mariana: Third-Grade One-Way DLBE Teacher

Background

Mariana was a third-grade teacher with 10 years of teaching experience in two different schools, both within the large urban district of this study. In the first school, she taught pre-K, kindergarten and first grade for eight years. At the time of the study, she was in her second year teaching at Maple Elementary (pseudonym), which was approximately 92% Hispanic, 96% economically disadvantaged and 57% of students were labeled English language learners (ELLs).

Mariana self-identified as Latina, female and bilingual. She grew up in Monterrey, Mexico, and pursued her teaching degree at the Tec de Monterrey. Her home language was Spanish. Shortly after graduating, she moved to the United States to teach in a bilingual program; she was recruited because of a shortage of bilingual teachers in the state. At the time of the study, she was in her fourth year of pursuing an online doctorate in education.

Mariana believed the DLBE program should be implemented with fidelity. She connected the success of the program to fidelity: 'mientras se siga y se respete lo que se está pidiendo del programa sí es efectivo [*as long as one follows and respects what the program is asking for, it is effective*]'. She was also theoretically aligned with the additive goals of bilingualism and biliteracy. When describing the DLBE implementation, she explained, 'It helps the students maintain their native language, learn academic language, and learn a second language at the same time through math and students' interactions and academic language'. However, Mariana articulated multiple logistical issues with the model. She felt the program had more requirements than the previous bilingual program and required more work, citing the extensive requirements for bilingual centers and word walls as examples. Thus, while Mariana recognized the importance of fidelity to the program, she simultaneously acknowledged the challenge of the additional requirements and even acknowledged making modifications to the model herself because 'no hay suficiente tiempo para poder hacer todo lo que se pide [*there is not enough time to do everything it asks*]'. The next section will examine the language policy Mariana embodied in her classroom, including how different school policies ultimately resulted in her inability to implement the model with fidelity.

Classroom language policy

It's 10am and the classroom schedule displayed on the wall indicates that it is social studies, but Mariana is still teaching math. Mariana finishes describing the instructions in English, and her twelve students begin working on a problem in their English test preparation manual. Mariana walks around and provides assistance to students that are stuck.

Karina is playing with a rubberband at her seat and as Mariana walks by she re-directs her saying, 'Deja esa por favor. Ponte a trabajar [Leave that alone please. Get back to work]'. Mariana circles around the table and crouches down next to Manuel. In a low voice, she begins to walk Manuel through the problem, 'Acuerdate que tienes que multiplicar antes de sumar [Remember that you need to multiply before adding]'. As she stands back up, she reminds the entire class in English that they have only 5 minutes left to finish problems 1–5. When the time is up, Mariana tells students in English that they will go over the problems tomorrow, but that it is time for English language arts. Ten of the twelve students shuffle to get their books together and line up at the door. Mariana instructs them in English that they may leave to go to their individualized tutoring. Only two students remain in Mariana's classroom who received high enough scores on the English reading practice tests to not be at risk of failing. She sits down with them at a small table and begins reviewing standardized test problems on reading.

Mariana worked in a self-contained third-grade classroom. She had 12 students, 8 boys and 4 girls. She described her students' linguistic proficiencies and said, 'La mayoría ahorita en español están entre medio y alto y en inglés también. No tengo niños que están empezando, todos están en intermedio o avanzados o alto. [*The majority right now in Spanish are medium and high and in English, too. I don't have children that are starting, they are all in intermediate or advanced or high.*]'. Mariana said that all students in the classroom were going to be tested in math in English and reading in Spanish corresponding to the language of instruction in the model. Mariana positioned her students in positive ways. Even when Mariana discussed students struggling with a concept or having a socio-emotional issue, she framed the discussion in a positive way or provided a counter-narrative.

Mariana voiced support for the district's DLBE program and language policy and enacted important parts of the model. However, additional factors influenced Mariana's classroom language policy and language practices. As illustrated in the opening vignette, central among these factors was standardized testing. While the model required Mariana to teach science and social studies in Spanish, her school administrators asked her not to teach these subjects, or to teach them minimally starting in January to accommodate the high-stakes State of Texas Assessments of Academic Readiness (STAAR) test preparation. Originally, Katy intended to complete all of her observations in Mariana's classroom in March and April, but Mariana told her that her administrator would not allow Katy in the classroom for the weeks leading up to and the week of the STAAR exam. As such, Katy completed classroom observations in March and May. The school climate and culture placed a high degree of stress and importance on standardized testing.

The priority placed on standardized testing had additional consequences for students. Mariana started every day by having the students run two laps around the outdoor track. However, only 6 of her 12 students participated, because 6 students spent the morning period receiving test preparation instead. In addition, as illustrated in the foregoing teaching vignette, 10 of Mariana's 12 students were taken out of the classroom for Spanish test preparation during English language arts. Only two students were identified as having high enough scores to ensure passing and could thus remain in the class. Mariana engaged these two students in test preparation during this time anyway. Test preparation consisted of completing practice test questions. Multiple layers of problematic language policy decision-making occurred during this spring semester; the large number of 'low' students pulled-out for test preparation resulted in a higher teacher–student ratio in the support classroom than in Mariana's classroom. This also implied student segregation, essentially tracking, and limited opportunities for peer scaffolding. What's more, the only two students exempt from test preparation were nonetheless engaged in school-mandated rote test preparation. Mariana was quite aware of the counterproductive nature of these mandates and their impact on her instruction. She explained:

> Hay presión por los exámenes y hay un momento en que no más nos enfocamos en prepararlos… trabajar en parejas cambiamos para enfocarnos más en las estrategias de lectura o de matemáticas [*There is pressure for the exams and there is a moment in which we only focus on preparing them… we trade our time working in pairs to focus more on reading and math strategies*].

As she described it, the testing pressure resulted in a period of time in which the third-grade team of teachers did nothing else but focus on the test. The pedagogical implications of this were clear and heartbreaking for the children. The DLBE model included interactive teaching strategies – learning in groups is crucial for language development and is an essential component of successful DLBE. But these strategies, including pair work and group activities, were not compatible with Mariana's school's approach to test preparation, which focused on teaching test-taking strategies to individual students. When she talked about 'reading and math strategies', Mariana was not actually talking about reading, or solving math problems, but rather about mastering the particular kinds of reading or math questions they would encounter on the STAAR test.

Throughout Katy's observations, Mariana was consistent in her language practices; they varied based on the subject she was teaching. Mariana generally followed the model and taught math in English, science in Spanish (observed in May after STAAR testing was completed) and a one-hour block each of both English and Spanish language arts, although as mentioned, almost all of the students were pulled out of the classroom for English language arts to receive Spanish language arts test preparation instead. When Mariana taught in Spanish (science or language arts), she rarely deviated from Spanish. During two observed science lessons (following the STAAR exam in May), Mariana showed BrainPOP videos (www.brainpop.com) in English. Despite the video presentation in English, Mariana kept the discussion in Spanish. In the retrospective interview, Katy asked Mariana about her use of English videos during science and she said, 'Porque no los tenemos (videos) en Español... pero la plática, todo de ciencias, sí es en Español. No más que sí, de repente los videos sí son algunos en inglés. [*Because we don't have them (videos) in Spanish... but the discussion, everything in science, is in Spanish. It's only that yeah sometimes a few of the videos are in English.*]'. Mariana attributed her use of English videos to lack of materials, which was an issue of program implementation in the interview analysis. The technique of showing a video in English and having a discussion in Spanish mirrors a translanguaging pedagogy – the intentional use of students' bilingualism as a resource for meaning making – technique (Celic & Seltzer, 2011). While Mariana did not frame her classroom instruction in this way, both the teacher and students were translanguaging (see Chapter 6 for more discussion on translanguaging and translanguaging pedagogy).

On the other hand, when Mariana taught in English (math) she shifted into Spanish much more frequently. We identified two patterns in Mariana's translanguaging shifts: (a) redirecting student behavior; and (b) clarifying a math concept with a student one-on-one.

Both of these patterns were illustrated in the opening vignette. In the following three examples, Mariana was instructing math in English and switched to Spanish to say, 'Deja esa. Ponte a trabajar. [*Leave that alone. Get to work.*]', 'Sientate Armando por favor [*Please sit, Armando*]' and 'Juan, te estoy hablando [*Juan, I am talking to you*]'. In each case, the teacher redirected individual students. In the third example, she actually told Juan, 'I'm talking to you' twice, before switching to Spanish and repeating 'Juan, te estoy hablando [*Juan, I am talking to you*]'. Similarly, Mariana switched to Spanish to clarify or help individual students. In every math class observation, students worked independently on practice problems for a period. During this time, Mariana was observed switching into Spanish to explain something to a student who had a question or was struggling with a problem. Also, a teacher's aide would come in to work with two students during this period, and she too was observed speaking in Spanish with the students.

Mariana created two additional instructional spaces in her classroom in which students were given the choice to engage in Spanish or English. When students returned from lunch, there were about 15 minutes before the 10 students were pulled out of the classroom for English language arts. During this time, Mariana had students write in a daily journal; she told them they could write in any language they wanted. During one observation, Katy noted that three students wrote in English and nine students wrote in Spanish. This was consistent with what Mariana described in a retrospective interview: she said there were three students who generally chose to write in English, while the rest chose Spanish.

The second opportunity students had to choose to use either Spanish or English was during independent reading. Mariana was dedicated to creating an environment that encouraged reading through student choice. She collaborated with the librarian and parents to ensure access to high interest books. During independent reading time, unlike journal writing, the students' language choices seemed to lean more toward English. On one occasion, nine students were observed reading in English and three in Spanish. This choice was mediated by the fact that more of the reading material, including one popular magazine specifically, was only available in English.

In addition to these two designated translanguaging instructional spaces, students appeared to have agency to choose their language of writing in the content area subjects too. For example, during one math lesson, the teacher passed out a worksheet with a blank graph. The students were asked to come up with questions they could ask to poll their fellow classmates, for example, 'What is your favorite animal: (a) cat; (b) dog; (c) horse'. The teacher did not specify the language for writing; some students wrote in English (which was the language that Mariana delivered the lesson in), but a majority wrote in Spanish. When students surveyed their classmates, similarly, the majority of the talk was in Spanish, although students also spoke some English. Mariana appeared to be supportive of students' translanguaging practices during math, engaging in translanguaging pedagogies to support their understanding, even as she maintained the language of instruction for actual whole group lessons.

Student oral language practices throughout the day involved a high degree of agency; they mixed Spanish and English language practices and used 'non-standard' varieties of both languages. Mariana was never observed explicitly correcting students' language or asking them to try to speak in English or Spanish. For example, students were observed multiple times using the English loanword 'la carpeta' in reference to the floor carpet. Mariana (who the reader will recall was raised and educated in Mexico) never reacted to this, nor corrected it.

In sum, Mariana strictly adhered to the language of instruction during Spanish, but was more flexible during English instruction. She also created two instructional spaces in which the students could choose the language in which they wanted to engage, and the majority of students chose Spanish. Students engaged in hybrid language practices orally and in writing. Ultimately, this created a classroom environment that was bilingual and slightly Spanish dominant. During the retrospective interview, when Katy shared her observation with Mariana that she spoke some Spanish in math, whereas she was not observed speaking English during Spanish instruction time, Mariana responded, 'Es inconsciente a veces. Sí trato de quedarme en el idioma y que los niños también me hablen en esa idioma. [*It is unconscious sometimes. I do try to stay in the language and that the children also speak to me in that language.*]'. After a long pause, she continued, 'Hay veces utilizo poquito español para explicarles, porque es más fácil para ellos en su idioma que en el inglés. Cuando veo que sí están batallando en matemáticas por ejemplo. [*There are times that I use a little Spanish in order to explain to them because it is easier for them in their language than in English. When I see they are struggling in math for example.*]'. Mariana originally recognized that some of her language choices were unconscious. As an initially Spanish-dominant speaker and Mexican national, it is likely that Mariana sometimes unconsciously switched to Spanish when she redirected student behavior. She also said that she tried to get students to speak to her in the language of instruction; however, this was never observed. Mariana also recognized that some of her choices were not unconscious – that sometimes she switched into Spanish to explain a concept with which the students were struggling. This was consistent with Katy's observations of her switching to Spanish when she worked one-on-one with students to explain something.

A Spanish-dominant third-grade classroom stood out to us, given our prior experiences in this district. Despite the explicit district-wide effort to implement DLBE, a transitional language ideology (the idea that students should be moved into English-only instruction as quickly as possible) was still very powerful throughout the district – and the push to transition students usually began in (or before) third grade. Yet, Mariana's classroom language policy choices (deliberate or not) fostered a highly bilingual and even slightly Spanish-dominant third-grade environment. Katy shared this observation with Mariana in the retrospective interview; she responded:

> De hecho nosotros decidimos, por ejemplo en los exámenes, si queremos que lo tomen en español o en inglés. Yo pedí que fuera todo en Español porque primero quiero que agilizan bien lo académico en español y luego ya si la maestra de cuarto quiere empujarlos para el inglés que ella los empuje al inglés. [*In fact, we decide, for example in the exams, if we want them to take it in Spanish or in English. I asked for it all to be in Spanish because first I want to well sharpen the academic in Spanish and then if the fourth-grade teacher wants to push them towards English than she will push them to English.*]

Mariana recognized that the role Spanish played in her classroom was at least, in part, the result of a specific language policy decision based on her own language ideology. She explained that she deliberately chose that her students would take the reading exam in Spanish, a decision based on her belief that the students should establish strong academic Spanish. Her description, including the words 'nosotros decidimos [*we decide*]', 'yo pedí [*I asked*]', 'si la maestra quiere [*if the teacher wants*]', depicted her school context as a place where teachers have agency to choose both language of instruction and language of testing. This agency appeared to empower Mariana to value academic Spanish, yet at the same time it allowed the fourth-grade teacher to 'empujarlos para el inglés [*push them towards English*]' if she wants. Where Mariana appeared to have no agency was the degree to which her instruction and curriculum was oriented around standardized test preparation. Mariana found spaces to enact agency and promote bilingual language development, yet she was fundamentally unable to implement the model with fidelity given the standardized test preparation demands. The next teacher case, Lisel, depicts the same struggle – but unfortunately with less teacher agency.

Lisel: Third-Grade Two-Way DLBE Co-Teacher (Spanish Side)

Background

Lisel identified as a Latina female in her early thirties. This was her first year at Woodward Elementary; however, she was in her ninth year teaching. Lisel identified as bilingual in Spanish and English. Both her parents spoke Spanish when she was growing up, and she attended school entirely in English. In this way, Lisel's bilingual upbringing resembled that of a large percentage of her students; she was a simultaneous bilingual who had been exposed to both Spanish and English prior to starting formal schooling.

Lisel co-taught two groups of children for the two-way dual language (TWDL) program alongside Rachel (Chapter 4) at Woodward Elementary. As described in Chapter 4, Lisel and Rachel's two classes were made up predominantly of initially Spanish-dominant students who were at different points along the bilingual/biliterate continua. Only 5 of the over 40 students were designated as 'native English speakers' across both classrooms (Hornberger, 2003). However, eight of the initially Spanish-dominant students were identified as stronger in English reading for their third-grade standardized assessment.

Lisel supported DLBE and articulated a desire to implement the program. She believed that bilingualism was an asset for children, and philosophically agreed that a DLBE program would serve her students. She also articulated that students should not mix languages and that code-switching was wrong. Lisel believed that it was okay to say one sentence in one language followed by a sentence in another language (intersentential code-switching/shifting); however, they should not be combined in a single sentence (intrasentential code-switching/shifting). Lisel's nuanced articulated language ideological perspective was not always embodied in her classroom, which we explore in the following classroom language policy section.

Although Lisel supported the DLBE program, she was more skeptical from the start about the ability to implement the model with fidelity. Lisel was concerned with the lack of professional development, shortage of materials in Spanish, time limitations and compatibility with STAAR preparation (Texas' standardized assessment). Her commitment to implement the program slowly faded over time during the first few months of the school year until by early spring she had completely abandoned it.

The struggle and slow abandonment of DLBE

Lisel and Rachel (Chapter 4) were co-teachers, but each implemented the DLBE program language policy very differently. Rachel was assigned to teach the English portion of the curriculum (math and English language arts) while Lisel was tasked with teaching the Spanish portion of the curriculum (science, social studies and Spanish language arts).

As described in Chapter 4, Rachel implemented the model with fidelity, instructing solely in English. She also followed the additional model requirements including implementing bilingual pairs and bilingual centers. As the next section describes in detail, Lisel did not implement the DLBE model with fidelity in her classroom; rather, she instructed in both English and Spanish. Before describing Lisel's classroom language policy, we provide some background information on the tensions that arose for DLBE implementation, and why Lisel gradually abandoned it altogether.

Lisel and Rachel met once a week with their grade-level team. The team had two additional members: Esmeralda, a one-way DLBE self-contained teacher, and Trisha, an English as a second language (ESL) generalist teacher who was not implementing the DLBE program. The weekly meeting was designated for the team to discuss issues of curriculum and instruction. At one of the first planning meetings in September, the principal attended and announced there would be an 'evaluation' of the DLBE program by consultants in the middle of October. It seems important to note that the Gómez-Gómez consultant team did not bill this first visit as 'evaluative' – the consultants billed their fall first-year visit as 'supportive', intending to give feedback to the teachers to improve their fidelity to the model and to answer any and all of the teachers' questions. Yet, the principal clearly framed it as evaluative to the teachers. In fact, across the district the visit was framed as evaluative.

The principal provided teachers with the checklist on which they would be 'evaluated', which included bullet points for the 'Dual Language Classroom Environment' and teacher pedagogy. The teachers only reviewed the 'Classroom Environment' portion of the checklist, the first half (left-hand side), because the Gómez-Gómez consultants' first visit would focus only on this portion. This included items related to classroom signage and organization, e.g. the expectation that labels be in blue for English and red for Spanish; the requirement to have two separate word walls posted, one in English and one in Spanish; the requirement that the classroom have separate areas for materials and signage related to each content area. This pretty much exclusive focus on the visual manifestations of DLBE for at least the first year of implementation had significant implications for how 'doing dual language' was co-constructed at the local level (Hornberger & Johnson, 2007; Menken & García, 2010). Teachers referred to this in our district-wide survey and interviews as well (see Chapter 3). Successful DLBE implementation appeared to mean adhering to a checklist of bullet points about such details as the presence of red and blue labels, the display of bins with color-coded journals, bulletin board displays of student writing and wall charts with students clearly paired by 'dominant' language. The lack of attention to teachers' actual curriculum, pedagogy or to the broader goals and ideological orientation of DLBE was problematic.

Multiple tensions surfaced throughout this initial planning meeting, further indicating a troubling start to the DLBE implementation. Most significantly, Esmeralda, the one-way DLBE teacher, expressed outright negativity toward the implementation; she was clearly not invested in the program. She argued with the principal throughout the meeting highlighting, for example, that she was worried about her students' test scores. She said, 'This (DLBE implementation) is additional stress. I just want to be responsible and worry and focus one hundred percent on my students'. For Esmeralda, this meant ensuring the highest test scores possible, which she felt was not compatible with the DLBE program. The argument escalated until the principal directly told her, 'You will do it. This is a requirement of the district'. 'Doing it' in this case appeared to mean making sure that her classroom had the visual aspects of the DLBE in place for the October evaluation.

Ultimately, as in other schools in which Deb observed, Woodward's teachers expressed that the visit in October was anticlimactic; they received little feedback and, of course, there were no consequences. Following the visit, the DLBE implementation was never the central topic of discussion again in all the planning meetings Katy attended. In fact, the teachers' conversations increasingly silenced any dialogue about children's bilingual/biliterate acquisition, about innovative or integrated learning or even about their students as individuals. Instead, teachers tended more and more toward discussion of what steps they needed to take in order to prepare their young students for the state's STAAR tests in math and reading.

In the few instances in the fall when the teachers did discuss issues that arose in DLBE implementation, noting particularly instances when the policy came into direct conflict with other district or state policies, including accountability policies, the tensions were always resolved in favor of testing and test preparation, regardless of whether such preparation ran counter to the DLBE program. For example, in October, Lisel was directed by the principal to implement 'Comprendo', an individualized computer drill/practice vocabulary development program during Spanish language arts. Lisel challenged the principal, asking, 'How does that fit into our bilingual research centers?'. She explained that she did not think individualized computer work fit with the DLBE program's bilingual research centers, which was a pedagogical practice of grouping children for project-based learning that was expected to happen in all Gómez-Gómez third- through fifth-grade classrooms. The principal clarified that Lisel needed to do the vocabulary development program, and that 'it was fine' to take children away from their bilingual research centers. In November, the conflicts increased. Lisel was directed to implement a reading preparation program on computer, called 'Achieve 3000'. It was clear that Achieve 3000 was a particular challenge to the DLBE teachers, because in order for it to best support students' preparation for the STAAR reading test, it had to be done 'in the native language', and it took upward of 45 minutes at a sitting to accomplish 'one article' on the program. Lisel was also tasked with implementing 'Motivations' reading during her Spanish language arts block, another reading test preparation program to be completed in the language the students would test in. From December to April, Lisel did not teach social studies or science in order to comply with the demands placed upon her for reading test preparation. Rachel began to ask Lisel about this in a planning meeting, 'So you spend the reading time, social studies time, and science time…' to which Lisel answered before she even finished the question, 'All Motivations [test practice]'. By the end of our contact with the teachers in mid-spring, there was no mention of DLBE program implementation during planning meetings. All conversation was around test preparation and administration.

Classroom language policy

To begin her Spanish language arts class, Lisel says 'Good morning, children. Get your motivation reading out'. Students scramble to take out their motivation reading standardized test preparation books. Lisel continues in Spanish, 'El grupo de Español, quiero que leen pasaje uno. El group de inglés quiero que leen lo que hicieron para la tarea [Spanish group, I want you to read passage one. English group, I want you to re-read what you did for homework]'. Lisel stops her instructions in Spanish, pausing to re-direct Juan Pablo in English, 'I asked you take out your book'. She then continues in Spanish, 'Quiero que todos leen el pasaje dos veces y van a subrayar cualquier palabra que no saben. [I want you all to read the passage two times and underline any word you don't know]'. Lisel walks around the room and monitors students who are reading silently at their desks. She does not check in with Gael, Marco, or Pedro who are sitting at a back table with a teacher aide. The teacher aide is guiding them individually through the motivation passage. Lisel also does not check in with Stacy and Mateo, two students who are sitting on bean bags in the corner of the room. Stacy and Mateo are reading the adolescent novel The BFG by Roald Dahl and Quentin Blake (1982). In the entire two-hour block very little changes. Lisel continues to switch between Spanish and English as she works through the Motivation reading. The teacher's aide continues to work one-on-one with her three students. Stacy and Mateo continue to read and work independently in the corner.

Lisel spoke in both Spanish and English during her designated Spanish language arts class. The following field notes were written during the first classroom observation: *When I walk in the classroom I am shocked to hear the teacher speaking in English* (November 2012). This was surprising because the TWDL model prescribed the teacher to speak and instruct solely in Spanish for Spanish language arts. This pattern held for all the classroom observations; the teacher spoke English and Spanish in all lessons. Students were also separated for distinct language practice (leveled Spanish or English) for at least part of every lesson except two. Between three and five students (identified as struggling learners) worked with a teacher's aide at the back of the classroom in Spanish.

Lisel used her designated Spanish language arts period as the time to complete her mandatory 'Motivation reading' program. Yet, students were required to complete their 'Motivation reading' in the language in which they were going to take their state test in April. Those eight students in the group who were identified to take their reading test in English – including two initially English-dominant students – were therefore provided workbooks in English, putting Lisel in the position of conducting whole-class instruction for students working in two different languages, in a classroom designated the 'Spanish side' of a two-way DLBE program, during the period reserved to focus on Spanish language arts. She resolved this by positioning students as belonging to the 'English group' or 'Spanish group'. For example, she said, 'Spanish group, put your homework away and you are going to do this part. English, get your motivation out' (1/30/13). In this example, the teacher provided instructions for both groups in English. In the foregoing vignette, she provided instruction for both groups in Spanish. Lisel rarely translated, thus despite labeling children as belonging to one language group or the other, she simultaneously positioned them all as competent bilinguals.

For the two final observations in April directly before standardized testing, six of the eight students who were identified to take the test in English were moved to the third-grade ESL classroom for test preparation in English. The two students who were not moved were the highest performing, and also the two initially English-dominant speakers. These were the two students (Stacy and Mateo) depicted in the vignette reading *The BFG* in the corner of the room. In an informal interview, Lisel explained that these students were not at any risk of failing the state test (STAAR), 'They would go. But they already got like 98% and we don't need to do that. No more test prep for you'. She further clarified that she didn't want to 'subject them to more STAAR preparation' (field notes 4/11/13), and so they completed an independent book study, hence these two students were reading books in English on beanbags in the corner of the room (during their Spanish language arts period).

The school's mandate that Lisel complete Motivation reading in two languages was a central reason for her constant switching of languages. In the following classroom observation, the students were reading a story from their workbooks, and Lisel attempted to negotiate students having the books in different languages:

1   **Lisel**: She's going to read it in English and you can read it in your mind in Spanish.
2   **Student 1**: (Student reads passage in English.)
3   **Lisel**: Melissa, will you read it in Spanish for us please.
4   **Student 2** (Student reads passage in Spanish.)
5   **Lisel**: Antonio, follow (strict tone). Rosa, *lea por favor* [Rosa, read please].

In Line 1, Lisel was speaking entirely in English, but asked students to 'read it in your mind in Spanish'. Lisel was negotiating how to instruct students using workbooks in two separate languages. Her negotiation continued in Line 3 when she asked a student in English to read it in Spanish. By asking the student in English, Lisel positioned the student as a competent bilingual; she expected the student to understand her English and read in Spanish. However, in Line 5, the teacher redirected Antonio in English and then in Spanish asked Rosa to read. This example illustrates how students engaged in more English or Spanish based on the language they were testing in; it determined what language they actually read in (Palmer, 2008).

In Line 5, it is possible the teacher switched into Spanish because she viewed Rosa as a more dominant Spanish speaker, although additional data analysis revealed an alternative explanation: Lisel would often switch between Spanish and English during classroom transitions and emotional responses (i.e. reprimand or praise). In the previous case, Lisel reprimanded Antonio in English and then switched to Spanish to ask Rosa to read. The following classroom examples further illustrate this pattern of the teacher linguistically shifting during an emotional response or a transition:

> *Me enojo más que no estás haciendo nada.* [It makes me more angry that you aren't doing anything.] (Pause) Cassandra, you are really testing my patience.

> We are going to do another one when you get back and I hope that you do better. *Imagínate si esto fuera la MOY* [Middle of Year Benchmark Test] *que van a tomar la semana que entra. ¡Nada más cuatro niños habrían pasado!* [Imagine if this was the MOY that you are going to take next week. Only four kids would have passed!]. (February 2013)

> (Following a question asked in Spanish and a student response in Spanish) Oh! That is a good inference! Okay, *¿cómo se siente Beatriz?* [Okay, how does Beatriz feel?]. (March 2013)

> Good morning, children. (Students say 'Good morning, Ms. C.'.) Get your motivation reading out. (Followed by seven turns by Lisel in Spanish.) (January 2013)

In each of the examples, Lisel shifted intersententially between Spanish and English language practices. In the first example, the teacher was speaking in Spanish to Cassandra and switched into English as she reprimanded her. In the second example, the teacher spoke initially in English and switched to Spanish as she reprimanded students in reference to their middle of the year (MOY) benchmark test scores. In the third example, the teacher guided students in a question-and-answer session in Spanish but switched into English to praise the student and then back into Spanish for more questions. In the final example, the teacher transitioned to start class using formulaic speech in English. Directly following the transition, the teacher began classroom instruction in Spanish.

Lisel generally shifted language practices intersententially; she would complete an entire sentence in Spanish or English before changing languages. However, in the previous example, Lisel said, 'Okay, *como se siente Beatriz?*'. Indeed, Lisel frequently said 'okay' while speaking in Spanish. The word *okay* was used as a filler word. While initially Spanish-dominant speakers more commonly use a word in Spanish such as *pues*, Lisel's use of the word *okay* signified her fluid bilingualism.

There were other discrepant cases when the teacher shifted language practices intrasententially. This occurred when the teacher appeared to change her mind or make a mistake. For example, in the process of instructing students to open their books to a particular page, Lisel said, 'Okay, *página* [page], wrong book' (November 2012). In another instance, Lisel was asking students questions and said, '*Yo uso* [I use], hold on, let me start my sentence again' (January 2013). Although these discrepant cases occurred in low frequency, the fact that she shifted language practices intersententially represented the embodiment of a particular language ideology that contradicted Lisel's articulated language ideology. We observed Lisel reprimand or redirect students on multiple occasions for shifting language practices intersententially, as demonstrated in the following example:

1   **Student**: *Mi hermana esta enferma y no tiene que ir a la escuela.* [My sister is sick and she didn't have to go to school.] *Está* lucky.
2   **Lisel**: *Suertuda.* [Lucky.] *Tu hermana es suertuda.* [Your sister is lucky.] *Acuérdate que el inglés y el español no se pueden mezclar.* [Remember that English and Spanish can't mix.]

Lisel articulated her disapproval of 'mixing' languages, despite her own constant intersentential shifting of language practices and occasional intrasentential shifts.

Lisel's language ideologies, i.e. accepting some bilingual practices (intersentential shifts) but not others (intrasentential shifts), potentially explained the spaces in the classroom for student language practices. Lisel was unable to implement a language policy in which certain bilingual practices were okay whereas others were not; students were observed speaking English, Spanish and shifting language practices to Lisel. Although Lisel redirected students on occasion to not mix languages within sentences, students were observed numerous times shifting language practices intrasententially in interactions with the teacher. Indeed, Lisel articulated her frustration with shifting language practices in a planning meeting: 'Go and get their language straight. No code-switching!' (October 2013). Lisel's inability to limit language mixing can potentially be explained by the combination of her embodied language ideology (she occasionally shifted language practices intrasententially) and the complexity of the language policy.

Unlike in Rachel's classroom from Chapter 4, where students appeared to engage in Spanish and translanguaging discretely, students fluidly shifted between languages in Lisel's classroom. In other words, the language ecology of Lisel's classroom was entirely hybrid in nature (Gutiérrez, Baquedano-López & Tejeda, 1999). Students were also observed speaking English, Spanish and shifting language practices with their classmates in Lisel's classroom. Indeed, peer interactions did not appear to differ substantially from classroom to classroom.

Discussion

Teacher agency, multiple policy demands and program investment

In both of these teachers' cases the structural issue of standardized testing pressure and corresponding language policy demands were overwhelming and individual agency, identity and investment were overpowered. In the case of Mariana, despite her articulated commitment to implement the DLBE program with fidelity, classroom observations revealed that she did not teach all of the content areas and spent the vast majority of her math and Spanish language arts block engaging in individualized test preparation. These were language policy decisions mandated by her administrators, which, in this case, superseded the district DLBE policy. Nonetheless, Mariana still made spaces for linguistic flexibility over the course of the day. She was able to find the 'wiggle room' (Erickson, 2004) to provide safe spaces for students to make meaning and assert agency in their linguistic choices.

Similar to Mariana, Lisel also articulated support for the program; however, she never discussed her desire to implement it with fidelity. Lisel worked on a grade-level team with another team member who prioritized standardized testing; Lisel's classroom language policy reflected this culture. Her ideologies did not compel her to push against it, and ultimately, she bought into the priority of achieving the highest test scores over bilingual development, relegating all social studies, science and Spanish language arts time to test preparation. Thus, unlike in Mariana's classroom, Lisel's bilingual language practices were predominantly mediated by students standardized test preparation materials being in two different languages. Lisel adapted her instruction to meet the needs of students taking the exam in English and in Spanish. While Lisel was against language mixing, 'No code-switching!', she did not embody this language ideology in her classroom. Her students engaged fluidly in both languages, suggesting that a teacher's embodied language ideologies can be more powerful than his/her articulated language ideologies.

As noted at the start of this chapter, DLBE research highlights the importance of investment (Freeman, 2004; Lindholm-Leary, 2001; Pérez, 2004) across different stakeholders. Mariana and Lisel both lacked support and investment from co-teachers and administrators. Mariana shared that her administrator told her not to teach social studies and science leading up to the STAAR exam and her students were pulled from her class for individualized STAAR preparation. Lisel's administrator mandated that the third-grade team implement the DLBE model, but simultaneously asked Lisel to implement the Motivation reading test preparation program for each student in their 'native language'. Lisel's administrator was unaware the she was not teaching social studies and science; however, Lisel felt that her responsibility was to prioritize test preparation for her students to pass the exam. With respect to co-teachers, Mariana noted that the fourth-grade teacher at her school would likely transition students to English-only and one of Lisel's grade-level team members, Esmeralda, was outwardly against the implementation. Lack of school-wide investment in the DLBE implementation contributed to Mariana and Lisel's struggle to implement it.

Nevertheless, Lisel's co-teacher, Rachel (Chapter 4) implemented the model with fidelity, which merits some additional attention. This drastically different outcome and degree of agency to implement the DLBE model alongside standardized testing appeared mediated by two key factors. First, Lisel was implementing the Spanish portion of the curriculum whereas Rachel was implementing the English portion. The responsibility for test preparation was not shared across teachers; it was the time for Spanish language arts instruction that was compromised, highlighting a larger structural issue of English dominance. In other words, English hegemony supported Rachel's ability to teach in English, while Lisel's Spanish instruction was compromised (Gramsci & Hoare, 1971; Pavlenko, 2002). The other influential factor was the language of assessment. It was decided that some of Lisel's students would take the reading assessment in Spanish and others would take the reading assessment in English. Whereas it was decided that all of Rachel's (Chapter 4) students would take the math standardized assessment in English. As a result, all of Rachel's student materials were in English, and she did not need to creatively navigate a classroom space the way Lisel had to with students engaging in the same curriculum, but in two different languages. Meanwhile, in the other case, Mariana made the significant policy decision to test all of her students in Spanish. This might have been the key factor why Mariana, in contrast with Lisel, was able to create a slightly Spanish-dominant space in her classroom. Across all three cases, the decision about standardized test language functioned as *de facto* language policy (Menken, 2008; Nero, 2014; Shohamy, 2006).

Tension: Bilingual DLBE implementation vs monolingual standardized testing

One complication for DLBE program implementation was the sociopolitical school environment that emphasized standardized testing accountability. Since the passage of the federal law *No Child Left Behind* (NCLB 2001), which included a mandate for annual standardized testing of all children nationwide in Grades 3 through 8, the United States has increasingly institutionalized a standardized testing system linked to severe consequences for schools, teachers and students deemed low performing (Meier & Wood, 2004). ELL students are particularly vulnerable (Abedi, 2002, 2004; Gándara & Rumberger, 2009; McNeil & Valenzuela, 2001; Solano-Flores & Trumbull, 2003). The high-stakes consequences of NCLB have been shown to support test-centered instruction (Kohn, 2000) and exert curricular control (Au, 2007; McNeil & Valenzuela, 2001; Sloan, 2005). In Texas, these accountability controls have been in place significantly longer. High-stakes single-measure accountability is deeply rooted in school systems and in the educational philosophies of public school educators and school leaders; it is not uncommon to find schools with high numbers of ELL-designated students implementing extreme measures like those described in Lisel's and Mariana's schools in an effort to ensure adequate numbers of passing scores. The 2015 renewal of NCLB, known as the *Every Student Succeeds Act* (ESSA), did little to change this. For these two teachers, as for many others across the state and country, standardized testing narrowed their curriculum – taking out social studies and science and reducing math and literacy instruction to test-related materials – and shifted their pedagogical choices such that children moved from interactive, project-based participation spaces to individual rote practice of test-taking skills.

This educational policy climate presents a precarious situation for bilingual education, in which teachers are expected to instruct in two languages while they and their students are only held accountable to demonstrate content knowledge in one (Menken, 2008; Palmer, 2008). In other words, the additive goals of DLBE, bilingualism, biculturalism and biliteracy conflict with accountability pressure to perform well on monolingual exams. At the same time, and with no small measure of irony, members of DLBE communities have a tendency to rely on the scores of DLBE students (as compared to students in non-bilingual programs) to provide legitimacy and future advocacy for DLBE programs (Pérez, 2004). Ultimately, teachers become the key local language policymakers to negotiate this tension, and they can feel obligated to dedicate time to testing, taking away from content instruction (Pérez, 2004). For Mariana and Lisel, the administrative and school climate of testing pressure restricted their agency, and the DLBE implementation suffered or was abandoned altogether. Chapter 6 presents two teachers who, in comparison to Mariana and Lisel, were more successful in implementing DLBE, but unlike Marisol and Rachel in Chapter 4, made significant model adaptations.

Discussion Questions

(1) How can teachers ensure students succeed on standardized tests alongside DLBE program implementation?
(2) Reflect on your own experiences with test taking and test preparation. To what extent has this institutionalized educational practice been normalized in your own schooling and teaching experiences?

6 Teacher Cases: Adapting the Model or Valuing Linguistic Hybridity in DLBE

Across the district, teachers adapted the model to fit their local classroom context. As described in Chapter 3, teachers across the district made comments highlighting their role as a policymaker and describing modifications they made to their classroom based on their beliefs and context. These teacher adaptations to the model varied in scope and meaning from minor (changing the structure of the word wall) to major (changing the language of instruction for a content area). These model adaptations articulated by teachers connected to the structural issues for the top-down dual language bilingual education (DLBE) implementation regarding the student population and who the model served (or did not serve). Teachers made comments about the model working or not working because of a specific population and described the program either meeting or not meeting their population's needs.

The two teacher cases in this chapter did not believe that the model's strict separation of language worked for their bilingual classroom. As a result, the teachers presented as cases in this chapter did not implement the model's language separation for content instruction with fidelity, but instead engaged in translanguaging pedagogies – the intentional use of student bilingualism as a resource (García, 2009a). Theoretically, translanguaging goes beyond codeswitching, which arguably implies languages as two separate codes (García, 2009a). In order to validate and harness the everyday language practices and meaning-making processes of bilinguals, translanguaging emphasizes a single linguistic repertoire (García & Wei, 2014; Otheguy *et al.*, 2015). Spanish–English bilingual children engage in a variety of language performances to make sense of their bilingual worlds – including named practices such as 'English', 'Spanish', 'Spanglish' and 'codeswitching' – all of which can be considered to fall under the umbrella term of 'translanguaging'. The individual linguistic repertoires of the students include features that defy the boundaries of externally imposed, socially constructed named languages (Otheguy *et al.*, 2015). Importantly, translanguaging validates and normalizes this range of bilingual performances, including those that have been historically stigmatized.

This chapter contributes to the current wave of research on translanguaging, including how it can be used in educational settings as a pedagogical tool for language and content learning (Blackledge & Creese, 2014; Cook, 2001; García, Johnson & Seltzer, 2017; Horst *et al.*, 2010; Zentella, 1997). In this chapter, we highlight the connection between the participants' identities and language ideologies and their creation of classroom spaces that valued language hybridity. At the end of the chapter, we discuss the implications for translanguaging pedagogy and the central tension of teachers' navigating a policy implementation that does not align with his/her teaching experience or ideologies.

Olivia: Pre-K One-Way DLBE Teacher

Background

Olivia taught pre-kindergarten at Hillside Elementary. At the time of the study, she had been at the school for 10 years. Prior to Hillside Elementary, she worked for two years at a public school in the same district that was implementing a Montessori DLBE program. When, for various reasons, this program was discontinued, Olivia moved to Hillside to teach in its transitional bilingual education program. The community at Hillside was predominantly Latino with families of low socioeconomic status, although implementation of the two-way DLBE strand at Hillside had already begun to shift school demographics with a new population of white affluent students (this trend continued; see Heiman, 2017).

At the time of the study, Olivia was implementing the one-way DLBE program. All students were supposed to speak and understand Spanish for admittance to the program. All students except one were Latino and described as initially Spanish-dominant speakers. However, it was clear to Olivia that students were at different points on the bilingual continua (Hornberger, 2003). She described students' proficiencies as varying based on their exposure to each language. Many of her students had been exposed to English and Spanish from birth (simultaneous bilinguals), while some students entered the pre-K program with minimal exposure to English. Olivia noted in particular that students with older siblings generally had higher levels of English comprehension and speaking skills. This chapter shows how Olivia took this linguistic variation into consideration for her classroom instruction.

Olivia is a National Board-certified teacher in early childhood and bilingual education, Montessori trained, and is extremely reflective about the materials and instruction she provides to her young students. Olivia is from the Rio Grande Valley and claims a bilingual, bicultural identity. In an interview, she said, 'I grew up speaking Spanish, but it was just a very natural thing, you know just being on the border you just did'. Her stance toward bilingualism, combined with her previous teaching experience in DLBE classrooms and her considerable preparation (with both a master's degree in bilingual/bicultural education and National Board Certification in early childhood and English as a second language [ESL]), positioned her as a master bilingual teacher among her peers.

Olivia went through the district's dual language professional development and heard about the expectations for separating the two languages of instruction within their academic program. Although she expressed some reservations about the training (e.g. 'the training was kind of quick'), she had read research about the positive potential of DLBE and was invested in the program (Collier & Thomas, 2004; Lindholm-Leary, 2001). She was determined to follow the model 'with fidelity', as expected by the district. In Olivia's words, 'I'm still learning about it but overall I think I have the gist of it. It's a good program, a good model'. In fact, according to Olivia, the school's entire faculty was committed to the program and determined to make it work. She explains:

> Last year when they were deciding what schools were going to be pilot schools, we had to apply. We had to, as a campus, complete the application together, faculty, all of us. So we all knew exactly what they were asking and what was expected and all of that... Everybody we know is on board and if they are not they should probably not be here. And they know that.

Despite Olivia's commitment to the model implementation, her classroom instructional choices involved adaptation of the model to her local context, which we explore in the next section.

Classroom language policy

Olivia and her pre-K students are sitting in a circle on the carpet. Olivia is modeling a math bilingual pair activity. She points out to her students in English that the activity is on a blue tray, so students should complete the activity in English. She repeats this instruction in Spanish.

On top of the tray is a blue bucket which contains five plastic hanging monkeys and a plastic crocodile. Olivia selects a student to help her complete modeling the activity asking, 'Can I have a bilingual student to help me act out this activity'. All of the students eagerly raise their hands. She explains in English that one bilingual partner should hold the hanging monkeys and the other student should hold the crocodile, pointing to the props as she explains. Olivia's students are already familiar with the 'Five Little Monkeys' song they will sing as they act out the activity. Olivia continues carefully and purposefully to model the student actions that go along with the song lyrics, 'When you sing, "And snapped that monkey out of the tree", the partner with the crocodile should use the crocodile to snap the bottom hanging monkey'. Students laugh in excitement. One student shouts out, 'El cocodrilo está comiendolo [The crocodile is eating it]'. Olivia responds, 'Yes, the crocodile is snapping the monkey out of the tree'. At this point in the demonstration, the school janitor enters the room. Olivia pauses the lesson and greets the janitor in Spanish. Her students similarly greet the janitor in Spanish. After the brief interruption, Olivia seamlessly transitions back to modeling the activity. Olivia models the activity two times through and demonstrates how you should switch turns holding the monkeys and being the crocodile. As the activity demonstration comes to a close, Olivia asks students, 'Does anyone have any questions o dudas de cómo hacer esta actividad? [or doubts about how to do this activity]'. She tells students that the new activity will be available to pick for their bilingual partner time. Students clap and shout out excited phrases in both English and Spanish, 'cool!' 'chido!'.

Olivia's classroom language practices modeled dynamic bilingualism. As demonstrated in the vignette, despite math being designated as an English instructional period, Olivia engaged purposefully in Spanish for student learning. She clarified instructions in Spanish and asked if students had questions in both English and Spanish. When the janitor – a Spanish-dominant speaker – entered the classroom, Olivia switched to Spanish. These linguistic shifts were counter to the official model. However, Olivia was arguably modeling the behavior of a fluent bilingual in ways that were supportive of her students' learning of context-appropriate language engagement.

The following interaction is an additional example of Olivia translanguaging in her classroom during a transition from whole-class instruction to learning centers time. Olivia is explaining to her pre-kindergarten students that she is closing one of the learning centers temporarily, so she can introduce new activities:

EXAMPLE 1: Modeling Translanguaging

Olivia:	This is going to be here for now ((showing the students a sign)). Stop. Pare. ['Stop'.] No venga, okay? ['Do not come, okay?'] Do not come to that center.
Student A:	How come on both sides?
Olivia:	I meant to write it only in Spanish and I did it in English too. (glances at researcher sheepishly)
Student B:	¿Por qué? ['Why?']
Olivia:	Because hay muchas cosas allí que los niños ya no están usando. ['Because there are a lot of things there the children are not using anymore'.]

Olivia begins speaking in English but switches to Spanish to repeat/translate 'stop'. She continues in Spanish but shifts intrasententially when she says 'No venga, okay?' and then translates her Spanish back into English. Olivia is modeling hybrid language practices as she shifts in and out of the two named languages in a seemingly effortless and natural manner. Both translations appear to serve the purpose of ensuring student understanding of these important directions (Zentella, 1997). When Student A asks Olivia in English why she has written on both sides of the sign, she responds to his question by looking at the researcher and admitting that she 'accidently' made the sign in both languages. She is clearly exhibiting her tension with the model of strict language separation. Her own hybrid language practices are not in alignment with such separation. Student B then asks Olivia (in Spanish), '¿Por qué?' inquiring why she is closing the learning center. When Olivia responds, she shifts intrasententially again, beginning in English and moving into Spanish. It is possible that she switches to Spanish in response to the students' Spanish language choice. Her move into Spanish might also be to ensure student comprehension. Although Olivia is aware that she is not supposed to be engaging in such language switching in her dual language classroom, she continues to carry on the language practices she believes will best facilitate understanding and development for her very young emergent bilingual students. This interaction was one of multiple exchanges illustrating the classroom's dynamic bilingualism. Despite the school's 'language of the day' policy that called for 'transition language' to be carried out in one specified language each day, classroom transitions were a clearly identified space for dynamic bilingualism in Olivia's classroom.

Olivia also positioned students as bilingually competent during classroom instruction and interaction. For example, as demonstrated in the vignette, Olivia would ask for a 'bilingual volunteer' and refer constantly to the students as 'bilingual partners'. Indeed, Olivia's work to position students as developing bilinguals began with her strategy of pairing students for their bilingual pair work. While the DLBE program prescribed that students be labeled English dominant or Spanish dominant and paired across language groups for collaborative work, Olivia viewed her students' language practices and identities in a more complex and dynamic way. According to the model, Olivia should have identified and labeled students by language proficiency for bilingual pair work at the beginning of the year. Olivia felt that partners should be determined based on multiple factors, including personality and academic strengths, as well as a more thorough linguistic profile of the students. She believed this could only be accomplished through getting to know her students, and thus required more time. Against the recommendations of the consultant team, Olivia did not begin bilingual pair work with her pre-kindergarten students until November, approximately three months into the school year. Olivia said:

> I need some time to just get to know my kids, get to know their personalities, get to know academically their levels and that kind of thing too because sometimes that quick little assessment test that we give them when they first come in to qualify for pre-K doesn't show anything. It's the first time they've met me. It's totally inappropriate... So I have to give them some time and I obviously have to do some more anecdotal observations type things in class... especially for the first month of school. Kind of to really know them academically and their personalities too. (Interview, April 2011)

When Olivia ultimately did make pairs, she took into account students' academic level, personality and language proficiencies, thus expanding upon the recommendations of the dual language program consultants. She explained:

> I'll put the person with the stronger English with the person that's a little bit weaker in English... there are kids that do prefer and I've noticed that they have been speaking a lot more English and they are speaking it well, so. Based on that, too, we try to pair them, you know English–Spanish speakers [with Spanish speakers].

Olivia took into consideration student preference and student language choices to develop bilingual pairs. She understood that these behaviors changed and did not always correspond to the dichotomous labels assigned to students including English language learner (ELL) and native English/Spanish speaker. So she used the term 'English–Spanish speakers' in an attempt to better describe the linguistic repertoires of particular students.

Olivia engaged in additional strategies to position students as bilingually competent and encourage them to invest in bilingual identities. One strategy was to ask students to translate for their classmates. In this short transcript, before the children choose their center activities, Olivia is explaining to them that if she has not taught them how to use a game with their partner, they are not to play with it. The interaction is with Anabel, a Spanish-dominant developing bilingual.

Olivia: You cannot get this until I show it to you. Can somebody say that in Spanish? Anabel puedes decir eso en Español? ['Anabel can you say that in Spanish?'] Can you say that? Tell your friends. (said with no pause)

Anabel: No puede agarrar quisita porque la señora nunca me moresta. ['You cannot take (invented word) because the woman never (invented word, possibly me muestra "show it to me")']

Olivia: That's right. Si tu maestra no te enseñó esto todavía no lo puedes agarrar. ['If your teacher did not show you it, you still cannot take it'.]

By asking, 'Can somebody say that in Spanish?', Olivia is positioning all the students in the classroom as potential language brokers, dual language experts and dynamic bilinguals. Olivia then specifically selects Anabel to provide the translation. Anabel is Spanish dominant but is developing her English language skills. When Olivia asks her to translate English into Spanish, she positions Anabel as a capable bilingual translator. After asking Anabel in Spanish if she can translate, she repeats her question in English, modeling translation. Before Anabel can respond to the yes or no question 'Can you say that?', she says without pausing 'Tell your friends'. With rising intonation on the word 'that' but no pause after it, Olivia manipulates the timing in this interaction to not allow for a 'no' response (Erickson, 2004). In this way, Anabel is further positioned as a student capable of translating the question. Indeed, the student's translation is expected regardless of her actual ability to translate the question. It turns out that she is actually not able to fully translate the question verbatim, although she seems to have captured the teacher's sentiment. Anabel's difficulty to produce an instant translation of the teacher's words echoes research that identifies translating as a complex cognitive task (Orellana, 2009). Yet, Olivia positively affirms Anabel's attempt to translate by saying immediately, 'That's right'. Through her teacher's positive reinforcement, Anabel is encouraged in the future to step into this role again. After affirming Anabel's answer, Olivia then translates the question into more conventional and broadly comprehensible Spanish, thus modeling for Anabel the language terms she seems to have not already known, modeling the value and importance of translating as a skill and ensuring that all students understand these important instructions for classroom participation.

The deliberate positioning of students as language brokers and translators occurred in Olivia's classroom regardless of the students' actual bilingual competencies, implying her use of positioning as a tool to encourage the development of bilingual competencies in the students. Our final teacher case is Michael, a third-grade bilingual teacher who similarly engaged in translanguaging instructional practices for student academic and linguistic development.

Michael: Third-Grade One-Way DLBE Teacher

Background

At the time of the study, Michael was a third-grade teacher with 13 years of teaching experience at the same school, Otter Elementary (pseudonym). Michael self-identified as white, male and bilingual. He grew up in central Texas, starting his schooling experience in the large urban district where he later became a teacher. He spent the majority of his educational experience in a rural area district outside the city. Michael first began to learn Spanish through going to elementary school with Spanish-speaking peers and going to work with his father who was a contractor with Spanish-speaking workers. He then started acquiring Spanish formally in eighth grade and majored in and obtained a bachelor's and master's degree in Spanish from two large universities in Texas. His formal training was supported by personal and professional experiences, including interacting with Spanish-speaking co-workers in construction and restaurants, playing music professionally in an Afro-Cuban/Flamenco group and serving as an interpreter for non-profits in Mexico, Cuba, Dominican Republic and Peru. These different experiences exposed Michael to different varieties of Spanish, particularly those of northern and central Mexico, as well as Dominican Spanish.

Similar to Olivia, Michael viewed student bilingualism and bilingual practices in complex way. Michael articulated pluralist language ideologies that differed from the vast majority of teachers we encountered in our four years conducting research in the district. Michael expressed a positive orientation toward linguistic hybridity as illustrated in the following quotes:

> Yo creo que hacer el 'code-switching' es algo muy functional. Es lo que hace la gente bilingüe siempre cada día. [*I think that doing 'code-switching' is something that is very functional. It is what bilingual people always do every day.*]

> (Spanglish) Es algo que es súper conocido en la cultura, incluso Adam Sandler hizo una película acerca de eso. [*It (Spanglish) is something super well-known in the culture, including Adam Sandler made a movie about it.*]

> Me encanta (Spanglish), sé que hay muchos que están a favor y en contra, pero si estamos hablando o haciendo chistes hay muchos recursos donde puedes crear cosas nuevas con el Spanglish. [*I love it (Spanglish), I know that there are many that are in favor and against it, but if we are talking and telling jokes there are a lot of resources where you can create new things with Spanglish.*]

Michael indicated that shifting language practices was both functional and normal. It is 'lo que hace la gente bilingüe siempre cada día [*what bilingual people do every day*]' and 'super conocido [*really well-known*]'. Finally, he offered his opinion on Spanglish: he loves it, but acknowledges that not everyone shares his opinion.

When this research was conducted, Otter Elementary was approximately 86% Hispanic, 93% economically disadvantaged and had an ELL population of 41%. Otter Elementary was officially implementing a one-way DLBE program. All of Michael's students were initially Spanish-dominant speakers and were at different points on a broad spectrum of bilingualism and biliteracy (Ballinger, 2013; Hornberger, 2003). The majority of Michael's students could be described as simultaneous bilinguals, having been exposed to both Spanish and English from birth, although some of Michael's students were immigrants with varying degrees of exposure to English based on when they immigrated and their language experiences prior to immigration.

Simply put, Michael did not comply with the DLBE program's language separation mandate that required Spanish be spoken while teaching science and social studies, and English while teaching math, with separate English and Spanish language arts blocks – nor with the administrative policy to transition students to English as quickly as possible. Over his 13-year tenure with the school district, he had become increasingly discouraged with policies that demonstrated contradictory messages, which ultimately led to assimilationist practices for Spanish-speaking students. He reflected that his decision to subvert the policies was rooted in parental support from the community and years of experience learning how to navigate the system and enact pedagogical practices in covert ways (i.e. switching to the linguistic expectation of the day whenever administrators or district personnel conducted walkthroughs). Michael also recognized that his positionality and subjectivity as an English-speaking white male contributed to his agency and emboldened his stance. Michael and the teacher with whom he team-taught in their departmentalized third-grade program felt that they owed it to the children and families to expose them to what it means to speak different varieties of English and Spanish as well as to maintain their first language. This stance was connected to their knowledge that the fourth- and fifth-grade teachers had highly distinct language ideological orientations and, upon leaving third grade, their students would be taught with the goals of transitioning to English. Michael also felt that a policy of language separation was not appropriate for new immigrants in his class. He explained:

> Creo que depende del contexto, de caso a caso. Dual lenguage pudiera funcionar, pero si llega un niño que no habla nada de inglés? Él necesita apoyo para poder no estar agobiado con esa situación. [*I think it depends on the context, from case to case, dual language could work, but if a child arrives not speaking any language? He needs support to not be overwhelmed in that situation.*]

For these reasons, Michael embraced a translanguaging educational policy that disrupted the designated language model and traditional ways of teaching (García, 2017; García & Kleyn, 2016). The next section offers a window into his pedagogical practices, particularly translanguaging shifts.

Classroom language policy

Lunch and recess have just come to an end, and students shuffle into Michael's classroom. Michael asks who is the 'comediante del día [comedian of the day]' and Pedro shouts out 'Soy yo! [It's me]' and assumes a position at the front of the class with a book of jokes in Spanish. Pedro reads the joke, '¿En qué se parecen una abeja y un elevator?' After a few student guesses, he shares, 'Los dos andan buscando de flor a floor'. After the classroom laughter dies down, Michael asks the students, 'What made the joke funny?' A student raises her hand and explains the double meaning of the word 'flor/floor' in English and Spanish. As the discussion about the joke comes to an end, Michael takes out his guitar signaling to students that they are transitioning to science and asks students, 'Would you like to sing first in Spanish or English?' Students shout out different choices 'Spanish!' 'English!' and Michael decides to sing the song first in Spanish. The song is about making inferences:

> *Busca la evidencia ['Look for the evidence']*
> *Y encontrarás la inferencia... ['And you will find the inference...']*
> *Aparece tu mamá y no se ve feliz ['Your*
> *mom appears and she doesn't look*
> *happy'].*
> *¿Cómo sabíamos? ['How'd we know?']*
> *Busca la evidencia ['Look for the evidence'].*

The class sings along to the Spanish version followed by the English version. Michael puts the guitar away and gives students a new set of instructions in Spanish to continue working on the observation of their crawfish. Students immediately go to work. They get with their science partner, get their crawfish from the science shelf, take out their science notebooks and begin to write down observations. Michael walks around the classroom checking in with students and asking them if they are seeing anything interesting. One student shares with Michael, 'El crawfish se echó pa'tras'. Michael writes the observation on the board. A student shouts out, 'Mister, you're writing in Spanglish'.

As illustrated in the vignette, Michael did not separate English and Spanish in his classroom instruction. Rather, he strategically used both languages for academic and linguistic development, for example singing content-based science songs in both English and Spanish (and letting the children choose). Indeed, in every classroom observation, Michael used Spanish, English and hybrid language practices. Michael's shifting easily and frequently between Spanish and English was the norm rather than the exception. For example, in the linguistic analysis of the first video, which was 15 minutes long, Michael moved between language practices associated with English and Spanish 26 times.

Michael's translanguaging shifts served multiple pedagogical purposes including accessing content, building community and developing metalinguistic awareness. Just like Olivia, Michael selectively translated during instruction and shifted language practices based on the interlocutor to ensure access to important instructions and content. He had cognate charts and key vocabulary translations posted on the wall that were constantly being updated and changed by both students and teacher. After introducing new vocabulary, he would often say the word, count down from three and have the students repeat the new vocabulary word. Michael also produced formulaic expressions that students would echo or repeat during instruction throughout the day in both Spanish and English to increase student access to content. Some of these formulaic phrases he introduced in a third or fourth language that was in the broader school community such as Bosnian and sign language. Introducing additional languages from the school into the classroom served to build community. Additional strategies involving translanguaging shifts to build community included mirroring student language choices and redirecting/praising in different languages.

Michael consistently made connections between Spanish and English. In fact, because of his own excitement about exploring language variation, he was constantly making connections between different varieties of Spanish and English. Drawing on strategies to develop students' metalinguistic awareness, he brought their attention to linguistic features. As illustrated in the vignette, Michael incorporated songs and joke/riddle-telling into his daily instruction. At the start of most science lessons, Michael would take out his guitar and sing the science song of the week in Spanish followed by English, or vice versa, sometimes depending on student choice. The singing ranged from being about content, such as chlorophyll or magnetism, to reinforcing scientific method and concepts, like the inference song example in the vignette. Some of the songs he translated himself, others he developed himself (including the inference song example presented in the vignette). Michael drew the students' attention to language features and bilingualism, thus enhancing their metalinguistic awareness, when he introduced songs. For example, in the excerpt in the vignette from the song that he composed about making inferences, the Spanish version borrows from the English lexicon to maintain the rhyme. Because Michael was unable to come up with a suitable Spanish word to rhyme with feliz ('happy'), he inserted 'sister' (pronounced ' seester'), which was a word that the majority of the class knew and became the students' favorite part of the song. The play with language shifting to bring across the meaning of the lyrics exhibited an additional manifestation of a translanguaging pedagogy, which the children easily and enthusiastically followed. By intentionally including both English and Spanish in a single song even though he was fully aware of the potential stigma attached to this. In particular, the administration of his school was strongly biased against language mixing. Michael was pushing back against both the historical marginalization of hybrid language practices and school language separation policy.

Michael also brought students' attention to language and engaged in translanguaging shifts during the daily joke-telling routine. Learning about and through humor can be an effective strategy for language learning (Bell, 2009). As Michael explained,

> I think jokes are one of the highest levels of language understanding.... If you can understand the double entendres and things of political, social, and cultural meaning, it is the highest level. The comedian has to pull from all different lexicons.

Michael went beyond modeling and engaging in translanguaging shifts; he directly taught students about linguistic variation. These conversations inevitably included translanguaging shifts as well. Michael's ongoing conversations about code-switching and Spanglish with his students fostered spaces for linguistic connections and the development of critical language awareness (Alim, 2010; Martínez, 2013). Michael consistently assured students it was 'okay' and 'normal' to mix languages, as they all engaged in this linguistic practice all the time. He also taught students about the differences between the regional Spanish used throughout Texas and the Spanish spoken in other parts of the world – for example, 'carpeta (*carpet*)' versus 'alfombra (*carpet*)', 'troca (*truck*)' versus 'camioneta (*truck*)' and 'pushar (*to push*)' versus 'empujar (*to push*)'. Similarly, he taught his students about dialectical differences in English in different parts of the country (i.e. west coast versus east coast) in terms of pronunciations within English such as aunt (/ænt/ or /ɑː nt/) and a horse's hooves (/hʊ vz/ or /huvz/). It was clear in the vignette that the students in this classroom were aware of language variation – when Michael was writing on the board, a student called out, 'Mister, you are writing in Spanglish'. The student pointed this out not to disparage it, but simply to point it out. This interaction was evidence of Michael's creation of a classroom space that fostered this type of metalinguistic awareness. In a retrospective interview, he explained why the student might have made this observation:

> We have used the word Spanglish before. We have talked that all bilingual people really mix, do that, codeswitch.... We don't have a negative connotation for that. All bilingual people that I have ever met, whether in a humorous way or just to come up with a word, code-switch.... We have definitely talked about the beauty of that.

Michael's ideological viewpoint and pedagogical approach valued the translanguaging practices of his students' families and communities, providing a counter-hegemonic perspective on the sometimes derogatorily used terminology of 'Spanglish' vernacular.

Michael's direct instruction on linguistic variation occurred within Spanish and English. On one occasion, Diego, a recent Honduran immigrant in Michael's class, worriedly told Michael on the way to lunch that he did not have any money to buy food by saying, 'Maestro, no tengo pisto' ['*Teacher, I don't have any money*'], to which some of Diego's Mexican peers began to giggle, whisper and respond, '¿Pisto?... ¿qué es eso?' ['*Pisto, what is that?*']. Michael turned the conversation around by asking his Mexican students in Spanish what they thought the word might mean in Honduran vernacular Spanish. Stumped by the question (and perhaps still fixating on the idea that Diego had potentially said a bad word because pistear means 'to drink alcohol' in some Mexican dialects), Michael explained that pisto was similar to saying lana (literally: wool; colloquially: money) in the Mexican variety of Spanish. The students marched on toward the cafeteria with a new lexical item in the class's linguistic repertoire. Michael had disrupted the potential miscommunication and misunderstanding and instead put explicit value – by giving it the attention of intellectual curiosity – on his new immigrant student's unique linguistic repertoire. In this way, he embraced an understanding of the social struggles surrounding the use of two or more languages, and the ways that we can shift power dynamics through everyday intentional interactions with bilingual students (García, 2017).

Discussion

Translanguaging, identity and agency

A new wave of scholars has taken up the call to develop bilingual instructional strategies that break away from the traditional dual–monolingualism paradigm (Creese & Blackledge, 2010; Cummins, 2005; García, 2009a; Gutierrez, Bien, Selland & Pierce, 2011; Lee *et al.*, 2011; Mori, 2007; Reyes & Vallone, 2007). We found that some bilingual teachers implementing DLBE in the district were already engaging in translanguaging pedagogy. Both Olivia and Michael modeled dynamic bilingualism and created classroom spaces for students to draw on their full linguistic repertoires. Olivia delayed assigning students' bilingual partners until she had gotten to know her students, and did not view their assigned language position (English versus Spanish model) as either fixed or binary as the program model seemed to be pushing her to do. Michael created classroom spaces for hybrid language practices through routines (joke-telling/ singing songs) that strategically used both Spanish and English. He also constantly made connections between English and Spanish which created opportunities for students to develop metalinguistic awareness.

Olivia and Michael both engaged in translanguaging pedagogy. Olivia felt that strict language separation was not always appropriate for her pre-kindergarten students, particularly at the beginning of the school year when they were still transitioning to school and she was getting to know their language practices, academic skills and personalities. Michael never strictly separated his Spanish and English language practices because he felt that it hindered access to content for all his students, and it was not appropriate for newly arrived Spanish-speaking immigrants in his classroom. On the contrary, he believed that the beautiful nature of bilingual languaging made a wonderful teaching tool. Olivia and Michael shared a pluralist language ideology and respect for their students' linguistic backgrounds that mediated their instructional choices and adaptation of the DLBE model.

Olivia and Michael's identities and prior experiences were linked to their pluralist language ideologies and influenced their classroom translanguaging pedagogy. The dynamic bilingualism displayed by Olivia was facilitated by her own experiences growing up in bilingual communities and households. This influenced Olivia's embodied instructional practice that went beyond mere acceptance of hybrid language practices to actually provide spaces in the classroom in which dynamic bilingualism was modeled and encouraged (i.e. switching languages to greet the janitor). As Olivia shared, engaging in bilingual practices was something 'you just did' growing up in South Texas. Michael's identity and experiences also intimately connected with his pluralist ideological translanguaging stance. As an initially English-dominant, white male, Michael likely never experienced discrimination based on his language practices. Similar to other white, initially English-dominant speakers who communicate in a second language, he had always been praised for his Spanish-speaking skills. His valuing of translanguaging practices, including features associated with Spanglish, was intertwined with his positive experiences when engaging in these language practices himself. An individual with a different subjectivity, such as a teacher of color who engaged in the exact same language practices, could be stigmatized, perceived as unintelligent and/or discriminated against (Flores & Rosa, 2015; Rosa, 2018). Michael asserted, moreover, that shifting back and forth freely between languages outside of formal learning environments had always been a part of his language practices and experience.

Both teachers consistently allowed, valued and even mirrored students' voices and linguistic choices. Olivia and Michael both worked in DLBE contexts where the majority of students were simultaneous bilinguals having been exposed to both English and Spanish language practices from birth. Such instructional practices might be particularly appropriate in a context in which linguistic hybridity is pervasive (Valdés, 2005). The two teachers in this chapter took the time to assess their students' language practices and drew on this knowledge for their classroom pedagogy.

Tension: Implementing policy mandates vs instructing in ways that align with experience and ideology

As discussed, Olivia and Michael's experience and ideology did not fully align with classroom language policy of strict language separation as prescribed by the DLBE model. Both teachers had to navigate this tension and, ultimately, both teachers enacted teacher agency and adapted the model to fit their local context. We contend that the main source of Olivia and Michael's agency came from their many years of teaching experience and levels of expertise. Olivia selected to work at Hilltop because she knew it would be a supportive environment for developing student bilingualism and biliteracy. Olivia could explain her instructional choices based on her years of experience working with this student population and her extensive experiences and education, including National Board Certification and a master's degree in bilingual/bicultural education from a reputable university in the area. Her decisions were respected by her colleagues and principal; she was viewed as an expert bilingual teacher. Michael did not work in a supportive school environment for student bilingualism. His administrators advocated for teachers to transition students to English as quickly as possible. However, Michael's 13 years' experience, his master's degrees in Spanish linguistics and his own subjectivity as an initially English-dominant white male afforded him the ability to subvert both the district and school language policy; he had figured out ways to 'work the system'. Other teachers, particularly educators from oppressed groups or those with fewer years' experience or less formal education, would be taking a bigger risk to resist mandated policies, particularly teachers working in unsupportive school environments.

Discussion Questions

(1) In what ways did Olivia and Michael promote language development alongside valuing dynamic bilingualism and bilingual identity formation?
(2) How does teacher agency connect to DLBE program implementation?

7 Discussion and Conclusions: Implementing DLBE to Serve Emerging Bilinguals

Without a doubt, implementing dual language bilingual education (DLBE) programs is a complex, multifaceted and long-term project. In truth, any top-down implementation of any kind of policy on a large scale in schools is inevitably messy and complicated; it is simply in the nature of the phenomenon for things to go differently than planned. And, even on the relatively smaller scale of a single school, implementation of a DLBE program is inevitably messy and complicated. When it comes to language in education policy, well-laid plans always seem to go awry. On the other hand, plans are not everything, and 'awry' is in the eye of the beholder; teachers' agency and professional judgement have the potential to bring to the table unanticipated opportunities and open up spaces for unique kinds of learning. Whenever thoughtful, critically engaged, professional educators are involved, education spaces are filled with opportunity for hope and possibility for positive change.

All of the teachers presented in this book were working in the same school district, with the same mandated DLBE model; yet, it is very obvious that their classroom language policies and practices varied tremendously. If one is focused entirely on the issue of fidelity, one might call this a fail; but these were all thoughtful, caring teachers, deeply involved in the project of educating young emerging bilinguals for futures filled with possibility. Reflecting on the situations each teacher found himself/herself in, it is possible to see some of these classrooms as more successful spaces than others. What can we take from examining these cases as a whole that might support new DLBE programs as they work to ensure equity and excellence for emerging bilingual learners? Each chapter identified a tension that is widespread and prevalent in the implementation of DLBE programs.

In Chapter 4, we highlighted a tension – prevalent in DLBE contexts – between implementing a model 'with fidelity' and valuing and developing classroom spaces for *bilingual* development. Both Marisol and Rachel worked hard to implement this DLBE model with fidelity. Their efforts protected spaces for bilingual development – an important and critical part of DLBE programs – yet, at the same time, in their efforts to follow a recipe they had been given, they limited spaces for dynamic bilingualism and hybrid language practices. This is a tension that DLBE teachers struggle with in many contexts, within the dictates of many different DLBE program models and under the guidance of school and program leadership that run the gamut of beliefs about bilingualism.

In Chapter 5, we explored the tension around implementing DLBE programs that promote bilingualism and biliteracy within a sociopolitical climate that emphasizes monolingual standardized test preparation. The two teachers in Chapter 5, Mariana and Lisel, struggled to implement the model given the pressures they faced to ensure their students succeeded in high-stakes tests. Again, this is a tension that is prevalent throughout bilingual education in the US context; it is hard to envision a way to make monolingual testing an equitable or fair experience for bilingual children, especially in the elementary school years. Adding high stakes to that equation means that bilingual programming tends to suffer – as it did in Mariana's and Lisel's classrooms – as educators strive to ensure their students (and their schools) survive the system.

Finally, in Chapter 6, we unearthed the tension of teachers navigating a district policy mandate that did not fully align with their ideology and experience. Olivia and Michael drew on their more extensive teaching experience and relatively high level of professional capital to enact their agency in the face of mandates, and to thoughtfully and creatively adapt the model to their local contexts. Their examples provide hope that professional agency can, in a sense, mediate policy in positive and transformative ways that center students' needs. Yet, given their unique professional positions, it is clear we cannot simply say, 'do as they do' – many teachers are not in the privileged position to agentically flaunt mandates, at least not without significant supports, and without the level of experience that Olivia and Michael possess it is not clear we would always want them to.

So, what messages can be drawn from examining this set of cases? What ideas apply to other contexts? Drawing on our cumulative research in this district and beyond, and reflecting more broadly on the experience of observing the messiness of both top-down and grassroots attempts to implement DLBE, we venture to make some recommendations to those who wish to ensure they are implementing strong, equitable and empowering DLBE programs for emerging bilingual students. We hope these ideas can support any language in education policy implementation, whether a small strand program in one school or an entire district or state-level implementation:

- Program investment, including a clear space drawn for exploratory, innovative practices protected from high-stakes testing.
- Careful attention to the role of language ideologies at different levels (program, classroom and individual educator) of policy implementation.
- Consideration of the language practices of students and the need for a program model and classroom spaces that allow children to both use and grow their language, including historically minoritized and marginalized practices.
- Promotion of teacher professionalism and agency.

In this final chapter, we will tackle each of these recommendations, discussing the implications for teachers, administrators and researchers.

Program Investment and Protection from High-Stakes Testing

As Hornberger and Johnson (2007) point out, any language policy implementation is messy and multilayered, as it will inevitably involve negotiating a range of ideologies, resources and interpretations at every level; it should not be surprising that the teachers faced challenges as they worked to make such drastic changes to their bilingual program's structure, function and goals. It is also not surprising that implementing change on a large scale and in a top-down process poses even more challenges. High-stakes accountability, though, seems to magnify these challenges – to make individuals' ideologies more difficult to shift, to draw resources away from the kinds of material and time investments necessary for success, to distract and confuse teachers as they attempt to make sense of the various demands.

Top-down DLBE program implementation must not be confused with top-down *support* for DLBE implementation. If anything, these six cases and the district-wide interview data suggest that alignment between school, district and program policies is crucial for DLBE implementation; top-down support is key. While this district at its highest levels (i.e. the superintendent and the director of multilingual services) officially endorsed the bilingual/biliteracy goals of DLBE when they adopted the Gómez and Gómez model for DLBE, local implementation of the program became obscured by ubiquitous and deeply entrenched monoglossic standardized testing policies. Many administrators in this large urban district who served in roles in the intervening levels between the superintendent and the teachers in their classrooms, themselves had minimal training or understanding of the DLBE model or research/ practice in the education of emergent bilingual students. Thus, without much understanding of the new initiative to implement DLBE in bilingual schools, these leaders continued to follow business as usual, expecting schools to 'transition' students into English instruction in time for testing deadlines and/or to organize their schedules to ensure coverage of mandated (monolingual) curriculum or test-preparation materials. As a result, teachers often faced conflicting, incompatible messages and mandates, and while mandates related to DLBE implementation may have been affiliated with stronger, more positive practices for their emerging bilingual students, the mandates related to ensuring high test scores came with strong systems of rewards and consequences. It is not surprising that in many situations these mandates prevailed; what might be more surprising (and what gives us hope) was that so many of our teacher participants were actually able to navigate the conflicts, to advocate for DLBE, maintain bilingual instruction and support biliteracy development for their young students.

Rather than attempt, as this district did, to implement the same monolithic DLBE program in every school at once, district stakeholders interested in providing enrichment bilingual programs would likely benefit from allowing schools to select and/or design program models that fit their local needs. Then, they would need to invest deeply in professional development for both teachers and leadership, and flatten leadership structures to allow teachers with the most understanding of bilingual education and biliteracy development to have the agency to assert their judgement. In this way, bilingualism and biliteracy might have a chance to prevail.

Even in the best of circumstances, however – even with administrative and leadership support at all (or most) levels and local teacher/principal agency during the implementation process – inevitably, troubling mixed messages or counterproductive mandates will be conveyed to teachers whenever there is high-stakes accountability at play (Au, 2007; McNeil & Valenzuela, 2001; Palmer & Snodgrass-Rangel, 2011; Sloan, 2005). Educational leaders committed to DLBE program implementation should address this challenge with different stakeholders directly, and explicitly prioritize bilingualism and biliteracy over monolingual test preparation. As a field, we need to address the damage high-stakes testing does to bilingual programs and bilingual students at the state and national level.

We need to convince policymakers and the general public to support more productive, valid and equitable multi-measure assessment systems for *all* students, but especially bilingual students; and to move away from punitive, monolingual accountability. Without this systemic change, we question the chance for successful and ongoing implementation of DLBE on any kind of large scale. If 'success' for schools, teachers and students is narrowly defined as high scores on a single monolingual, monoglossic standardized test, educators' decisions will continue to reflect this goal rather than students' bilingualism, biliteracy and cross-cultural competence.

Attention to the Role of Language Ideologies

The critical role of language ideologies within DLBE implementation has been well established in previous research. Over a decade ago, Freeman (2004: 82) argued for what she viewed as the central issue for implementing the DLBE program: 'The real challenge is destabilizing established language ideologies and replacing them with alternative language ideologies'. Following this argument, Freeman appealed to local educators including administrators, parents and teachers to be active in creating new language policy in line with the ideological underpinnings of additive programs. We believe the cases we've described provide additional support for the important role of ideologies in the implementation of DLBE. Ideologies are complex; the combination of teachers' own language ideologies, and the prevalence of dominant societal ideologies, operated to mediate classroom language policies and create (or not) spaces for different types of classroom language practices. These cumulative findings have important implications for DLBE implementation.

Teacher language ideologies mediating classroom language policy

Synthesizing across the six teacher case studies, there is evidence for ways in which the teacher language ideological orientation mediated the local classroom language policy. Both Marisol and Rachel from Chapter 4 articulated additive language ideologies toward bilingualism, which influenced their personal investment in the program and the extent of their efforts to implement the model with fidelity. Marisol's additive language ideology connected to her personal experience of subtractive bilingual schooling as a child. Rachel, a sequential bilingual, articulated her commitment to bilingual education based on her experience that learning a second language can help bridge cultures and bring together diverse communities. Marisol's and Rachel's language ideologies mediated their classroom language policy in other ways. Marisol articulated an ideology of language standardization and described language mixing as a problem. As a simultaneous bilingual, Marisol engaged in these practices herself, and actually articulated a negative view toward her own language practices, describing herself as strong in neither language. This ideology of language standardization mediated her significant language policy decision to recommend that her student (Marco) who frequently engaged in Spanglish exit the bilingual education program entirely. Rachel similarly embodied an ideology of language standardization through enforcing strict language separation. Her classroom language ecology involved students engaging in bilingual language practices, but either covertly or occasionally overtly as a form of resistance.

Mariana from Chapter 5 constructed Spanish-dominant spaces in her classroom that were mediated by her language ideological orientation. Mariana accepted her students' diverse language practices, and allowed students to draw on their full linguistic repertoires for classroom activities. She articulated a strong belief in the importance that her students develop Spanish, and faith in her students' linguistic abilities; this connected to her identity as a Mexican national. Based on these articulated language ideologies, she made the significant language policy decision that all her students would take their State of Texas Assessments of Academic Readiness (STAAR) standardized exams in Spanish. As a result, she was able to create a third-grade classroom environment that was – at least in some ways – Spanish dominant.

Finally, in Chapter 6, Olivia and Michael's positive language ideological orientation toward linguistic hybridity resulted in a classroom language policy that was inclusive of a wide range of diverse language practices. Olivia and Michael both made classroom language policy decisions that centered their students' needs. Olivia engaged in bilingual language practices that reflected her own identity and background growing up in South Texas. She shifted her language practices when engaging with different people, expected her students to do the same and positioned them as competent bilinguals. Michael centered his students' academic and linguistic needs by focusing on access to content and teaching new language practices and metalinguistic awareness accordingly. When tasked with cognitively demanding tasks in one language, Michael explicitly told his students to draw on all their linguistic resources for meaning-making. His language ideologies connected to language learning instinctively led him to constantly make connections across languages rather than separate them. Without a doubt, teachers' own language ideologies influenced their classroom language policies.

Dominant societal language ideologies mediating classroom language policy

It was also evident in these teachers' classrooms the ways in which dominant language ideologies impacted DLBE implementation *despite* teachers' language ideological orientations. Chapter 5 demonstrated how dominant monolingual ideologies embedded within standardized testing negatively impacted and even derailed the DLBE program implementation despite teacher investment in the program. English hegemony seeped into classroom policies and practices in other ways. Lisel (Chapter 5), for example, articulated the importance of bilingual education; yet as the 'Spanish side' of the model, she was tasked with carrying the bulk of the reading standardized test preparation, whereas the space for English development was protected. Prioritizing English development within the DLBE implementation reflected the broader societal ideology of English dominance. Both Mariana (Chapter 5) and Michael (Chapter 6) made classroom language policy decisions that were mediated by circulating transitional language ideologies within the larger school community, again reflecting societal English dominance. Both Mariana and Michael discussed how their students would likely experience limited Spanish instruction upon leaving third grade. Mariana acknowledged that the fourth-grade teacher might 'push' the students to English. Michael more directly stated that the fourth- and fifth-grade teachers at his school differed ideologically and taught with the goal to transition students to English as quickly as possible. As a result, both Mariana and Michael deliberately created classroom spaces for Spanish: Mariana engaged in Spanish-only during content classes in Spanish, and engaged in some Spanish language practices during content classes in English. Students in Michael's classroom always explicitly had access to Spanish language practices for meaning-making. In other words, Michael and Mariana made explicit classroom language policies to challenge English dominance and the transitional mentality. We wonder how their classroom policies and practices might change if situated in a school truly invested in DLBE.

Complexity and teacher identity in the role of language ideologies in DLBE

It is important to acknowledge that the relationships between articulated and embodied teacher language ideologies were multiple and complex. Some teachers articulated an ideology that was different from what they embodied in the classroom. For example, Marisol (Chapter 4) articulated an ideology of language standardization and discussed code-switching and Spanglish as a problem, yet she was never observed correcting or redirecting these language practices in her classroom. Other teachers embodied a particular practice indexing a particular ideological orientation in one activity and then different in another. For example, Lisel (Chapter 5) redirected students to not engage in hybrid language practices, but then, at times, engaged in hybrid language practices herself. Teacher language ideologies were multiple, reflecting both dominant societal ideologies and counter-hegemonic ideologies at different points in time.

Furthermore, the teachers' articulated and embodied language ideologies intimately connected to their identities and previous experiences. There are similarities between Marisol's (Chapter 4) and Lisel's (Chapter 5) language ideological orientation toward language hybridity, for example, that appear to have been grounded in the fact that both these teachers were raised as simultaneous bilinguals in Texas, and throughout their lives had heard negative messages regarding hybrid language practices and their own language skills in their heritage language. Lisel and Marisol both viewed students' 'language mixing' as a problem. Their classroom language policies included correcting and redirecting students 'not to mix', despite frequently engaging in linguistic hybridity themselves. Along these same lines, as a sequential bilingual having learned her second language essentially in monolingual spaces, Rachel viewed strict language separation as crucial to the development of students' 'second' language, and the decisions in her classroom reflected this belief. Meanwhile, both Michael and Olivia had had opportunities, through master's degree programs focused on asset-based orientations toward language and language varieties, to interrogate their own language ideologies. Both stood on firm ground having developed deeper understandings of the value and richness of the range of linguistic practices their students brought with them into the classroom, and this was illustrated in the opportunities they both provided to their students to engage as bilinguals.

Life histories and experiences shape ideologies, and ideologies in turn shape practices. Teachers need explicit opportunities to reflect upon their beliefs around language and language practices, in order that these links can be deliberate and intentional, and in order to ensure teachers are best able to support students' bilingualism and biliteracy development from asset-based perspectives.

Implications for DLBE implementation

Districts and schools attempting to implement a DLBE program, particularly within top-down contexts, must begin to address the role of language ideologies systematically and deliberately at all stages of DLBE implementation. Ideological work needs to begin well before the DLBE program is implemented, along with the articulation of the goals, planning and preparation process, and the selection of a DLBE model. The district we studied appeared to adopt the DLBE program for its bilingual schools with the central purpose of raising standardized test scores. It should not be that surprising that the dominant language ideologies of monolingualism, English hegemony and the hegemony of standard language practices that are embedded in so many aspects of our society seeped – or flooded – into DLBE classrooms. The goals of DLBE implementation, as articulated by the Center for Applied Linguistics' 'Guiding Principles for DLE' should be for students to attain bilingualism and biliteracy, academic achievement and cross-cultural competence (Howard, Lindholm-Leary *et al.*, 2018). We align with scholars who argue for the need to add a fourth goal of 'critical consciousness for all' (Cervantes-Soon *et al.*, 2017). Of course, research has demonstrated that strong, well-implemented DLBE programs can result in higher test scores (Lessow-Hurley, 2013; Lindholm-Leary, 2005; Rolstad *et al.*, 2005; Steele *et al.*, 2017). However, instructional decisions at all levels need to be grounded in the shared goals of bilingualism, biliteracy, cross-cultural competence and critical consciousness (Cervantes-Soon *et al.*, 2017). The irony is, if higher test scores supplant the central goals in DLBE, then the implementation process is compromised, and ironically that same focus on test scores – and the embedded monolingual ideological orientation that comes with it – will ultimately undermine students' performance on the tests.

The implementation process for strong, enrichment-oriented DLBE programs is never completed. Even if a district has discursively centered their goals around bilingualism, biliteracy, cross-cultural competence and critical consciousness in their processes, ongoing thoughtful discussion about the DLBE model and the language ideologies embedded in the model must continue. Instructional practices need to be continually interrogated and renewed. A relevant example is the common practice of grounding DLBE program models in a language separation paradigm. While teachers, schools and even districts or statewide policies may have important reasons for demanding that instruction take place in only one language at a time, educators must acknowledge and grapple with the fact that this practice runs counter to current understandings of bilingual languaging, and that an increasing number of students in DLBE programs are simultaneous bilinguals whose home language practices regularly and naturally mix across traditional named-language boundaries. Professional development for educators implementing DLBE needs to target language ideologies on an ongoing basis; these are complicated questions without easy answers, and only through ongoing dialogue can we effectively support emerging bilingual learners to meet the goals of DLBE.

Consideration of Student Language Practices

One set of language ideologies deserves particular attention in the efforts to successfully implement DLBE programs at scale: beliefs around the 'correctness' and 'incorrectness' of non-standard language practices. As we just articulated, children's home language practices often diverge from the standard language expectations of schools. In a context like Texas, where our participants teach, classrooms are predominantly made up of simultaneous bilinguals. In addition, increasing evidence points to a dynamic understanding of bilinguals – all bilinguals – not as 'two monolinguals in one' but as dynamic, holistic users of language practices across at least two 'named languages' (García, 2009b; García & Kleyn, 2016; Grosjean, 1982, 2010). How does a DLBE program, among whose stated goals is the development of strong bilingualism and biliteracy, ensure that students emerge with a positive conception of their own vernacular and hybrid language practices, while also mastering the 'academic registers' of 'both/all program languages'?

First of all, we would assert that every DLBE program and every teacher needs to grapple with this question, openly discuss and interrogate their own beliefs around this important issue and come to their own solutions. In so doing, we hope they will consider these ideas:

- Protecting spaces in their program models not just for learning minoritized languages, but also for bilingual languaging.
- Moving away from rigid or strict percentage guidelines that constrain teachers' instructional practices.
- Allowing students access to their full linguistic repertoires for content-driven academic tasks.
- Centering students, their families and their communities for academic and linguistic curricular and instructional decisions.
- Developing critical language awareness (Alim, 2010) at the classroom and school level across students, teachers and school leaders.
- Adopting the goals of bilingualism, biliteracy, cross-cultural competence *and critical consciousness for all* (Cervantes-Soon *et al.*, 2017).

Promotion of Teacher Professionalization and Agency

Teachers implementing DLBE models are important mediators of classroom-level language policy (Hornberger & Johnson, 2007; Johnson, 2010; Marschall *et al.*, 2011; Menken & García, 2010; Palmer, 2011;

Skilton-Sylvester, 2003; Stritikus & Garcia, 2000). Teachers negotiate and make sense of the different layers of language policy to develop classroom language policy (Hornberger & Johnson, 2011). It is clear from all of the foregoing recommendations that at the heart of strong DLBE implementation – regardless of scale – is a professional, engaged, thoughtful educator doing his/her work with agency and artistry. It is impossible to create high-quality bilingual classrooms without high-quality bilingual teachers.

In the midst of a large-scale implementation of any policy initiative, we can sometimes lose sight of the importance of each individual educator in the experience of each individual child. Our purpose here was to point out – by offering windows into six classrooms full of children and the teachers who guide them every day – that if we lose sight of the players, we lose the game. Perhaps the most important message of this book is to remember to support each teacher, to give him/her access to the most up-to-date tools for engagement and the latest information, to engage him/her in ongoing experiences that support professional reflection and growth. Only in this way can he/she make those moment-by-moment and larger decisions that benefit each child in his/her class. Committed and prepared professionals filling our schools is the only way to ensure positive schooling experiences for emerging bilingual children – whether in DLBE programs or not.

Guiding Questions for Dual Language Bilingual Education Implementation

We believe DLBE provides opportunities for positive change, and we support a range of initiatives and approaches at different scales toward this effort in different contexts. We anticipate and welcome push back as to how our portrait of a top-down district initiative in Texas differs vastly from the potential issues, needs, challenges and opportunities in a different context. For example, how is this book relevant to a French DLBE immersion program in Utah or a two-way DLBE Mandarin program in California? We would like to acknowledge that across these vastly different contexts there *will be* emerging bilingual and linguistically diverse students in the schools, districts and states implementing them. Thus, the following are some guiding questions that could be used to promote discussion and reflection for DLBE program implementation:

(1) How well does your DLBE program serve and center linguistically marginalized emerging bilingual students and their families?

(2) How does your DLBE program value and validate diverse language practices that include hybrid and non-standard ways of engaging bilingually?
(3) How does your DLBE program actively work to mitigate English dominance?
(4) To what extent do teachers at your school have the agency and preparation to make informed decisions regarding language policy to support their students' biliteracy development?
(5) How well protected is your DLBE program from the pressures of monolingual standardized test preparation?
(6) How does your DLBE program support and develop positive and affirming bilingual identities?

Final Thoughts

DLBE programs are rapidly growing in number across the country, in large part because of top-down, large-scale implementation initiatives. Even when well implemented, these programs are not free of problems – far from it. Many researchers (ourselves included) have uncovered inequities and problematics that most definitely need to be addressed. However, we still think we are justified in seeing the expansion of DLBE programs as a potential opportunity to improve the linguistic and academic experiences of bilingual and linguistically marginalized students. The vision behind our understanding of DLBE is bright and transformative; the discourse that surrounds it has the potential to be liberatory. We just need to get it right.

Our optimism for DLBE expansion is based on our interactions with bilingual teachers such as the ones in this book. We asked our participants, 'What is DLBE?', and what we learned through our research, and hopefully demonstrated throughout these chapters, is that what DLBE means is co-constructed by the local actors, and ultimately mediated by the classroom teacher. In a large-scale, top-down DLBE implementation context, language practices, language ideologies and local language policies will vary tremendously. By providing windows into different teacher classrooms, we hope that educators – across all levels and contexts – can engage in reflection through imagined dialogue with the teachers in the case studies of the kinds of language practices, ideologies and policy they want to articulate and embody. We feel more strongly than ever that to improve the educational experiences of linguistically marginalized students ultimately lies in the hands of teachers. To end, we want to recognize all of the educators across the country who are centering emerging bilingual students in the process of DLBE expansion, and hope this book contains useful information to continue this important and timely work.

References

Abedi, J. (2002) Standardized achievement tests and English language learners: Psychometrics issues. *Educational Assessment* 8 (3), 231–257.

Abedi, J. (2004) The No Child Left Behind Act and English language learners: Assessment and accountability issues. *Educational Researcher* 33 (4), 4–14.

Adesope, O.O., Lavin, T., Thompson, T. and Ungerleider, C. (2010) A systematic review and meta-analysis of the cognitive correlates of bilingualism. *Review of Educational Research* 80 (2), 207–245.

Alim, H.S. (2007) Critical hip-hop language pedagogies: Combat, consciousness, and the cultural politics of communication. *Journal of Language, Identity & Education* 6 (2), 161–176.

Alim, H.S. (2010) Critical language awareness. *Sociolinguistics and Language Education* 18, 205–231.

Alvesson, M. (2003) Beyond neopositivists, romantics, and localists: A reflexive approach to interviews in organizational research. *Academy of Management Review* 28 (1), 13–33.

Apple, M. (1990) *Ideology and Curriculum.* New York: Routledge, Chapman & Hall, Inc.

Au, W. (2007) High-stakes testing and curricular control: A qualitative metasynthesis. *Educational Researcher* 36 (5), 258–267.

Bakhtin, M.M. (1999) The problem of speech genres. In A. Jaworski and N. Coupland (eds) *The Discourse Reader* (pp. 121–132). London: Routledge.

Ballinger, S.G. (2013) Towards a cross-linguistic pedagogy: Biliteracy and reciprocal learning strategies in French immersion. *Journal of Immersion and Content-Based Language Education* 1 (1), 131–148.

Beirich, H. (2019) The Year in Hate: Rage Against Change. *Intelligence Report* (February 20). Southern Poverty Law Center. See https://www.splcenter.org/fighting-hate/intelligence-report/2019/year-hate-rage-against-change (accessed 5 December 2019).

Bell, N.D. (2009) Learning about and through humor in the second language classroom. *Language Teaching Research* 13 (3), 241–258.

Blackledge, A. and Creese, A. (2014) Heteroglossia as practice and pedagogy. In A. Blackledge and A. Creese (eds) *Heteroglossia as Practice and Pedagogy* (pp. 1–20). Dordrecht: Springer.

Blanton, C.K. (2005) *The Strange Career of Bilingual Education in Texas.* College Station, TX: Texas A&M University Press.

Calderón, M.E. and Minaya-Rowe, L. (2003) *Designing and Implementing Two-Way Bilingual Programs: A Step-by-Step Guide for Administrators, Teachers, and Parents.* Thousand Oaks, CA: Sage Publications.

Callahan, R.M. and Gándara, P.C. (eds) (2014) *The Bilingual Advantage: Language, Literacy and the US Labor Market.* Bristol: Multilingual Matters.

Cazabon, M., Lambert, W.E. and Nicoladis, E. (1999) *Becoming Bilingual in the Amigos Two-Way Immersion Program* (No. 11). Washington, DC: Center for Applied Linguistics.

Celic, C. and Seltzer, K. (2011) *Translanguaging: A CUNY-NYSIEB Guide for Educators.* New York: CUNY-NYSIEB/The Graduate Center, City University of New York.

Center for Applied Linguistics (2016) Dual Language Program Directory. See http://webapp.cal.org/duallanguage/ (accessed 5 December 2019).

Cervantes-Soon, C.G. (2014) A critical look at dual language immersion in the new Latin@ diaspora. *Bilingual Research Journal* 37 (1), 64–82.

Cervantes-Soon, C.G. (2018) Race, social justice, and power equity in dual language education. Report for Civil Rights Project, UCLA. See https://www.civilrightsproject.ucla.edu/research/k-12-education/language-minority-students/race-social-justice-and-power-equity-in-dual-language-education/Race-Power-in-DL-Edited-CervantesSoon-Report-11-26.pdf (accessed 16 October 2019).

Cervantes-Soon, C., Dorner, L., Palmer, D., Heiman, D., Schwerdtfeger, R. and Choi, J. (2017) Combating inequalities in two-way language immersion programs: Toward critical consciousness in bilingual education spaces. *Review of Research in Education* 41 (1), 403–427.

Chaparro, S.E. (2019a) But mom! I'm not a Spanish boy: Raciolinguistic socialization in a two-way immersion bilingual program. *Linguistics and Education* 50, 1–12. https://doi.org/10.1016/j.linged.2019.01.003

Chaparro, S. (2019b) School, parents, and communities: Leading parallel lives in a two-way immersion program. *International Multilingual Research Journal.* https://doi.org/10.1080/19313152.2019.1634957

Christian, D. (1994) *Two-Way Bilingual Education: Students Learning through Two Languages.* Washington, DC: National Center for Research on Cultural Diversity and Second Language Learning.

Christian, D., Montone, C., Lindholm, K. and Carranza, I. (1997) *Profiles in Two-Way Immersion Education.* McHenry, IL: Delta Systems.

Citrin, J., Reingold, B., Walters, E. and Green, D.P. (1990) The 'official English' movement and the symbolic politics of language in the United States. *The Western Political Quarterly* 43, 535–559.

Cloud, N., Genesee, F. and Hamayan, E. (2000) *Dual Language Instruction: A Handbook for Enriched Education.* Boston, MA: Heinle & Heinle.

Collier, V.P. and Thomas, W.P. (2004) The astounding effectiveness of dual language education for all. *NABE Journal of Research and Practice* 2 (1), 1–20.

Cook, V. (2001) Using the first language in the classroom. *Canadian Modern Language Review* 57 (3), 402–423.

Craik, F.I., Bialystok, E. and Freedman, M. (2010) Delaying the onset of Alzheimer disease: Bilingualism as a form of cognitive reserve. *Neurology* 75 (19), 1726–1729.

Crawford, J. (2004) *Educating English Learners: Language Diversity in the Classroom* (Vol. 5). Los Angeles, CA: Bilingual Education Services.

Creese, A. and Blackledge, A. (2010) Translanguaging in the bilingual classroom: A pedagogy for learning and teaching? *The Modern Language Journal* 94 (1), 103–115.

Cummins, J. (2000) *Language, Power and Pedagogy: Bilingual Children in the Crossfire.* Clevedon: Multilingual Matters.

Cummins, J. (2005) A proposal for action: Strategies for recognizing heritage language competence as a learning resource within the mainstream classroom. *Modern Language Journal* 89, 585–592.

Dahl, R. and Blake, Q. (1982) *The BFG.* New York: Farrar, Straus, Giroux.

Darling-Hammond, L. (1990) Instructional policy into practice: 'The power of the bottom over the top'. *Educational Evaluation and Policy Analysis* 12 (3), 339–347.

de Jong, E. (2011) *Foundations for Multilingualism in Education.* Philadelphia, PA: Caslon Publishing.

de Jong, E. (2013) Policy discourses and US language in education policies. *Peabody Journal of Education* 88 (1), 98–111.

DePalma, R. (2010) *Language Use in the Two-Way Classroom: Lessons from a Spanish–English Bilingual Kindergarten.* Bristol: Multilingual Matters.

Dorner, L. (2010) English and Spanish 'para un futuro' or just English? Immigrant family perspectives on two-way immersion. *International Journal of Bilingual Education and Bilingualism* 13 (3), 303–323.

Dorner, L. (2011) Contested communities in a debate over dual-language education: The import of 'public' values on public policies. *Educational Policy* 25 (4), 577–613.

Dual Language Training Institute (2018) Gómez & Gómez Elementary Dual Language Enrichment Model. See https://www.dltigomez.com/elementary-model.html (accessed 5 December 2019).

Eagleton, T. (1991) *Ideology: An Introduction.* London: Verso.

Emerson, R.M., Fretz, R.I. and Shaw, L.L. (2011) *Writing Ethnographic Fieldnotes.* Chicago, IL: University of Chicago Press.

Erickson, F. (2004) *Talk and Social Theory: Ecologies of Speaking and Listening in Everyday Life.* Cambridge: Polity Press.

Escamilla, K., Hopewell, S., Butvilofsky, S., Sparrow, W., Soltero-González, L., Ruiz-Figueroa, O. and Escamilla, M. (2014) *Biliteracy from the Start: Literacy Squared in Action.* Philadelphia, PA: Caslon Publishing.

Escobar, A.M. and Potowski, K. (2015) *El Espanol de los Estados Unidos.* Cambridge: Cambridge University Press.

Evans, B. and Hornberger, N. (2005) No child left behind: Repealing and unpeeling federal language education policy in the United States. *Language Policy* 4 (1), 87–106.

Fausset, R. (2019) Louisiana says 'Oui' to French, amid explosion in dual-language schools. *New York Times.* 21 August. See https://www.nytimes.com/2019/08/21/us/louisiana-french-dual-language.html (accessed 5 December 2019).

Fishman, J. (1969) National languages and languages of wider communication in the developing nations. *Anthropological Linguistics* 11, 111–135.

Fitts, S. (2006) Reconstructing the status quo: Linguistic interaction in a dual-language school. *Bilingual Research Journal* 30 (2), 337–365.

Fitzsimmons-Doolan, S. (2011) Language ideology dimensions of politically active voters: An exploratory study. *Language Awareness* 20 (4), 295–314.

Fitzsimmons-Doolan, S. (2014) Language ideologies of Arizona voters, language managers, and teachers. *Journal of Language Identity and Education* 12, 34–52.

Fitzsimmons-Doolan, S., Palmer, D.K. and Henderson, K. (2015) Educator language ideologies and a top-down dual language program. *International Journal of Bilingual Education and Bilingualism* 20 (6), 704–721.

Flores, N. (2016) A tale of two visions: Hegemonic Whiteness and bilingual education. *Educational Policy* 30 (1), 13–38.

Flores, N. and Rosa, J. (2015) Undoing appropriateness: Raciolinguistic ideologies and language diversity in education. *Harvard Educational Review* 85 (2), 149–171.

Freeman, R. (1998) *Bilingual Education and Social Change.* Clevedon: Multilingual Matters.

Freeman, R. (2004) *Building on Community Bilingualism.* Philadelphia, PA: Caslon Publishing.

Freire, J. (2016) Nepantleras/os and their teachers in dual language education: Developing sociopolitical consciousness to contest language education policies. *Association of Mexican American Educators Journal* 10 (1), 36–52.

Freire, J.A. and Delavan, M.G. (under review) Fiftyfication as a companion strategy for gentrifying dual language programs: Will 50:50-fits-all trample equitable language allocation?

Gal, S. (1998) Multiplicity and contention among language ideologies: A commentary. In B. Schieffelin, K.A. Woolard and P.V. Kroskrity (eds) *Language Ideologies: Practice and Theory* (pp. 317–331). New York/Oxford: Oxford University Press.

Gándara, P. and Baca, G. (2008) NCLB and California's English language learners: The perfect storm. *Language Policy* 7 (3), 201–216.

Gándara, P. and Rumberger, R. (2009) Immigration, language and education: How does language policy structure opportunity? *Teachers College Record* 111 (3), 750–782.

García, O. (2009a) *Bilingual Education in the 21st Century: A Global Perspective.* Malden, MA: Wiley/Blackwell.

García, O. (2009b) Emergent bilinguals and TESOL: What's in a name? *TESOL Quarterly* 43 (2), 322–326.

García, O. (2014) U.S. Spanish and education: Global and local intersections. *Review of Research in Education* 38 (1), 58–80.

García, O. (2017) Translanguaging in schools: Subiendo y Bajando, Bajando y Subiendo as afterword. *Journal of Language, Identity & Education* 16 (4), 256–263.

García, O. and Kleifgen, J.A. (2010) *Educating Emergent Bilinguals: Policies, Programs, and Practices for English Language Learners.* New York: Teachers College Press.

García, O. and Wei, L. (2014) Translanguaging and education. In O. García and L. Wei (eds) *Translanguaging: Language, Bilingualism and Education* (pp. 63–77). London: Palgrave Macmillan.

García, O. and Kleyn, T. (2016) *Translanguaging with Multilingual Students: Learning from Classroom Moments.* New York: Routledge.

García, O., Johnson, S. and Seltzer, K. (2017) *The Translanguaging Classroom. Leveraging Student Bilingualism for Learning.* Philadelphia, PA: Caslon Publishing.

García, O., Menken, K., Velasco, P. and Vogel, S. (2018) Dual language bilingual education in New York City: A potential unfulfilled? In B. Arias and M. Fee (eds) *Profiles of Dual Language Education in the 21st Century* (pp. 38–55). Bristol: Multilingual Matters.

García-Mateus, S. and Palmer, D. (2017) Translanguaging pedagogies for positive identities in two-way dual language bilingual education. *Journal of Language, Identity & Education* 16 (4), 245–255.

Genesee, F. (1987) *Learning through Two Languages: Studies of Immersion and Bilingual Education.* Cambridge, MA: Newbury House.

Genesee, F. (2001) Bilingual first language acquisition: Exploring the limits of the language faculty. *Annual Review of Applied Linguistics* 21, 153–168.

Genesee, F. and Lindholm-Leary, K. (2013) Two case studies of content-based language education. *Journal of Immersion and Content-Based Language* 1 (1), 3–33. doi:10.1075/jicb.1.1.02gen

Gkaintartzi, A. and Tsokalidou, R. (2011) 'She is a very good child but she doesn't speak': The invisibility of children's bilingualism and teacher ideology. *Journal of Pragmatics* 43 (2), 588–601.

Gómez, L., Freeman, D. and Freeman, Y. (2005) Dual language education: A promising 50-50 model. *Bilingual Research Journal* 29 (1), 145–164.

Gramsci, A. and Hoare, Q. (1971) *Selections from the Prison Notebooks* (Vol. 294). London: Lawrence and Wishart.

Grosjean, F. (1982) *Life with Two Languages: An Introduction to Bilingualism.* Cambridge, MA: Harvard University Press.

Grosjean, F. (2010) *Bilingual: Life and Reality.* Cambridge, MA: Harvard University Press.

Gutiérrez, K.D. and Rogoff, B. (2003) Cultural ways of learning: Individual traits or repertoires of practice. *Educational Researcher* 32, 19–25.

Gutiérrez, K.D., Baquedano-López, P. and Tejeda, C. (1999) Rethinking diversity: Hybridity and hybrid language practices in the third space. *Mind, Culture, and Activity* 6, 286–303.

Gutierrez, K.D., Bien, A.C., Selland, M.K. and Pierce, D.M. (2011) Polylingual and polycultural learning ecologies: Mediating emergent academic literacies for dual language learners. *Journal of Early Childhood Literacy* 11 (2), 232–261.

Haugen, E. (1959) Planning for a standard language in modern Norway. *Anthropological Linguistics* 1 (3), 8–21.

Heiman, D. (2017) *Two-Way Immersion, Gentrification, and Critical Pedagogy: Teaching against the Neoliberal Logic.* Austin, TX: University of Texas.

Heiman, D. and Yanes, M. (2018) Centering the fourth pillar in times of TWBE gentrification: 'Spanish, love, content, not in that order'. *International Multilingual Research Journal* 12 (3), 173–187.

Henderson, K.I. (2015) Dual language program implementation, teacher language ideologies and local language policy. Doctoral dissertation. See https://repositories.lib.utexas.edu/handle/2152/30925 (accessed 4 December 2019).

Henderson, K. (2019) The danger of the dual-language enrichment narrative: Educator discourses constructing exclusionary participation structures in bilingual education. *Critical Inquiry in Language Studies* 16 (3), 155–177. https://doi.org/10.1080/15427587.2018.1492343

Henderson, K. and Palmer, D. (2015a) Teacher scaffolding and pair work in a bilingual pre-kindergarten classroom. *Journal of Immersion and Content-Based Language Education* 3 (1), 77–101.

Henderson, K. and Palmer, D. (2015b) Teacher and student language practices and ideologies in a third grade two-way dual language program implementation. *International Multilingual Research Journal* 9 (2), 75–92.

Henderson, K. and Palmer, D. (2019) 'I wonder why they don't do the two-way': Disrupting the one-way/two-way dichotomy, re-envisioning the possibilities of dual language bilingual education. *NABE Journal of Research and Practice* 9 (1), 47–59.

Hill, J. (1998) Language, race, and White public space. *Anthropology & Education Quarterly* 100 (3), 680–689.

Hornberger, N. (2002) Multilingual language policies and the continua of biliteracy: An ecological approach. *Language Policy* 1 (1), 27–51.

Hornberger, N.H. (2003) *Continua of Biliteracy: An Ecological Framework for Educational Policy, Research, and Practice in Multilingual Settings*. Clevedon: Multilingual Matters.

Hornberger, N.H. (2006) Voice and biliteracy in indigenous language revitalization: Contentious educational practices in Quechua, Guarani, and Māori contexts. *Journal of Language, Identity & Education* 5 (4), 277–292. https://doi.org/10.1207/s15327701jlie0504_2

Hornberger, N. and Johnson, D. (2007) Slicing the onion ethnographically: Layers and spaces in multilingual language education policy and practice. *TESOL Quarterly* 41 (3), 509–533.

Hornberger, N.H. and Johnson, D.C. (2011) The ethnography of language policy. In T. McCarty (ed.) *Ethnography and Language Policy* (pp. 273–289). London: Routledge.

Horst, M., White, J. and Bell, P. (2010) First and second language knowledge in the language classroom. *International Journal of Bilingualism* 14 (3), 331–349.

Howard, E. and Sugarman, J. (2007) *Realizing the Vision of Two-Way Immersion: Fostering Effective Programs and Classrooms*. Washington, DC: Center for Applied Linguistics.

Howard, E., Sugarman, J. and Christian, D. (2003) *Trends in Two-Way Immersion Education: A Review of the Research* (No. 63). Baltimore, MD: Johns Hopkins University.

Howard, E.R., Lindholm-Leary, K.J., Rogers, D., Olague, N., Medina, J., Kennedy, B., Sugarman, J. and Christian, D. (2018) *Guiding Principles for Dual Language Education* (3rd edn). Washington, DC: Center for Applied Linguistics.

Hruschka, D.J., Schwartz, D., John, D.C.S., Picone-Decaro, E., Jenkins, R.A. and Carey, J.W. (2004) Reliability in coding open-ended data: Lessons learned from HIV behavioral research. *Field Methods* 16 (3), 307–331.

Johnson, D.C. (2010) Implementational and ideological spaces in bilingual education language policy. *International Journal of Bilingual Education and Bilingualism* 13 (1), 61–79.

Karathanos, K. (2009) Exploring US mainstream teachers' perspectives on use of the native language in instruction with English language learner students. *International Journal of Bilingual Education and Bilingualism* 12 (6), 615–633.

Katznelson, N. and Bernstein, K.A. (2017) Rebranding bilingualism: The shifting discourses of language education policy in California's 2016 election. *Linguistics and Education* 40, 11–26.

Kloss, H. (1998) *The American Bilingual Tradition*. Washington, DC: McHenry, IL/Center for Applied Linguistics/Delta Systems.

Kohn, A. (2000) *The Case Against Standardized Testing: Raising the Scores, Ruining the Schools*. Portsmouth, NH: Heinemann.

Kroskrity, P.V. (1998) Arizona Tewa Kiva speech as a manifestation of a dominant language ideology. In B.B. Schieffelin, K.A. Woolard and P.V. Kroskrity (eds) *Language Ideologies: Practice and Theory* (pp. 103–121). New York: Oxford University Press.

Kroskrity, P.V. (2004) Language ideologies. In A. Duranti (ed.) *A Companion to Linguistic Anthropology* (pp. 496–517). Malden, MA: Blackwell.

Lambert, W.E. (1975) Culture and language as factors in learning and education. In A. Wolfgang (ed.) *Education of Immigrant Students: Issues and Answers* (pp. 55–83). Toronto: Ontario Institute for Studies in Education.

Lee, J.S., Hill-Bonnet, L. and Raley, J. (2011) Examining the effects of language brokering on student identities and learning opportunities in dual immersion classrooms. *Journal of Language, Identity, and Education* 10 (5), 306–326.

Lessow-Hurley, J. (2013) *The Foundations of Dual Language Instruction*. Boston, MA: Pearson.

Lindholm-Leary, K. (2001) *Dual Language Education*. Clevedon: Multilingual Matters.

Lindholm-Leary, K.J. (2005) Review of research and best practices on effective features of dual language education programs. *Center for Applied Linguistics* 35, 17–23.

Lippi-Green, R. (1997) *English with an Accent: Language, Ideology, and Discrimination in the United States*. New York: Routledge.

López, M.M. and Fránquiz, M.E. (2009) 'We teach reading this way because it is the model we've adopted': Asymmetries in language and literacy policies in a two-way immersion programme. *Research Papers in Education* 24 (2), 175–200.

MacSwan, J. (2000) The threshold hypothesis, semilingualism, and other contributions to a deficit view of linguistic minorities. *Hispanic Journal of Behavioral Sciences* 22, 3–45.

MacSwan, J. and Faltis, C.J. (eds) (2019) *Codeswitching in the Classroom: Critical Perspectives on Teaching, Learning, Policy, and Ideology*. New York: Routledge.

Makoni, S. and Pennycook, A. (2007) *Disinventing and Reconstituting Languages*. Clevedon: Multilingual Matters.

Marschall, M.J., Rigby, E. and Jenkins, A. (2011) Do state policies constrain local actors? The impact of English only laws on language instruction in public schools. *Publius: The Journal of Federalism* 41 (4), 586–609.

Martin-Rhee, M.M. and Bialystok, E. (2008) The development of two types of inhibitory control in monolingual and bilingual children. *Bilingualism Language and Cognition* 11 (1), 81–93.

Martínez, R.A. (2010) Spanglish as literacy tool: Toward an understanding of the potential role of Spanish–English code switching in the development of academic literacy. *Research in the Teaching of English* 45, 124–149.

Martínez, R.A. (2013) Reading the world in Spanglish: Hybrid language practices and ideological contestation in a sixth-grade English language arts classroom. *Linguistics and Education* 24 (3), 276–288.

Martínez, R.A., Hikida, M. and Durán, L. (2014) Unpacking ideologies of linguistic purism: How dual language teachers make sense of everyday translanguaging. *International Multilingual Research Journal* 9 (1), 26–42.

McCollum, P. (1994) Language use in two-way bilingual programs. *IDRA Newsletter* 21 (2), 1–9.

McNeil, L. and Valenzuela, A. (2001) The harmful impact of the TAAS system of testing in Texas: Beneath the accountability rhetoric. In G. Orfield and M.L. Kornhaber (eds) *Raising Standards or Raising Barriers? Inequality and High-Stakes Testing in Public Education* (pp. 127–150). New York: The Century Foundation Press.

McQuillan, J. and Tse, L. (1996) Does research matter? An analysis of media opinion on bilingual education, 1984–1994. *Bilingual Research Journal* 20 (1), 1–27.

Meier, D. and Wood, G. (2004) *Many Children Left Behind: How the No Child Left Behind Act is Damaging Our Children and Our Schools*. Boston, MA: Beacon Press.

Meisel, J.M. (2007) The weaker language in early child bilingualism: Acquiring a first language as a second language? *Applied Psycholinguistics* 28 (3), 495–514.

Menken, K. (2008) *English Learners Left Behind: Standardized Testing as Language Policy*. Clevedon: Multilingual Matters.

Menken, K. (2009) No Child Left Behind and its effects on language policy. *Annual Review of Applied Linguistics* 29, 103–117.

Menken, K. and García, O. (2010) *Negotiating Language Policies in Schools: Educators as Policymakers*. New York: Routledge.

Menken, K. and Solorza, C. (2014) No Child Left Bilingual: Accountability and the elimination of bilingual education programs in New York City schools. *Educational Policy* 28 (1), 96–125.

Miles, M.B. and Huberman, A.M. (1994) *Qualitative Data Analysis* (2nd edn). Thousand Oaks, CA: Sage.

Miller, J. and Glassner, B. (1997) The 'inside' and the 'outside': Finding realities in interviews. In D. Silverman (ed.) *Qualitative Research: Theory, Method, and Practice* (pp. 99–112). London: Sage.

Mori, J. (2007) Border crossings? Exploring the intersection of second language acquisition, conversation analysis, and foreign language pedagogy. *The Modern Language Journal* 91, 849–862.

National Archives and Records Administration (1981, March 2) Remarks at the Mid-Winter Congressional City Conference of the National League of Cities. See https://www.reaganlibrary.gov/research/speeches/30281a (accessed 5 December 2019).

Nero, S.J. (2014) De facto language education policy through teachers' attitudes and practices: A critical ethnographic study in three Jamaican schools. *Language Policy* 13 (3), 221–242.

Nuñez, I. and Palmer, D. (2017) Who will be bilingual? A critical discourse analysis of a Spanish–English bilingual pair. *Critical Inquiry in Language Studies* 14 (4), 294–319. https://doi.org/10.1080/15427587.2016.1266266

Olson, K. (2009) Systemic reform and superficial compliance: Teacher loyalty to lived experience. *International Multilingual Research Journal* 3, 72–89.

Orellana, M.F. (2009) *Translating Childhoods: Immigrant Youth, Language, and Culture*. New Brunswick, NJ: Rutgers University Press.

Orellana, M., Ek, L. and Hernández, A. (1999) Bilingual education in an immigrant community: Proposition 227 in California. *International Journal of Bilingual Education and Bilingualism* 2 (2), 114–130.

Otheguy, R., García, O. and Reid, W. (2015) Clarifying translanguaging and deconstructing named languages: A perspective from linguistics. *Applied Linguistics Review* 6 (3), 281–307.

Ovando, C.J. (2003) Bilingual education in the United States: Historical development and current issues. *Bilingual Research Journal* 27 (1), 1–24.

Palmer, D.K. (2007) A dual immersion strand programme in California: Carrying out the promise of dual language education in an English-dominant context. *International Journal of Bilingual Education and Bilingualism* 10 (6), 752–768.

Palmer, D.K. (2008) Building and destroying students' 'academic identities': The power of discourse in a two-way immersion classroom. *Qualitative Studies in Education* 21 (6), 1–24.

Palmer, D.K. (2009) Middle-class English speakers in a two-way immersion bilingual classroom: 'Everybody should be listening to Jonathan right now…'. *TESOL Quarterly* 43 (2), 177–202.

Palmer, D.K. (2011) The discourse of transition: Teachers' language ideologies within transitional bilingual education programs. *International Multilingual Research Journal* 5 (2), 103–122.

Palmer, D. (2019) 'You're not a Spanish speaker!/We are all bilingual': The purple kids on being and becoming bilingual in a dual language kindergarten classroom. In C. Faltis and J. MacSwan (eds) *Code-Switching in the Classroom: A Multilingual Perspective on Language and Language Practices* (pp. 247–267). New York: Routledge.

Palmer, D. and Snodgrass Rangel, V. (2011) High stakes accountability and policy implementation: Teacher decision making in bilingual classrooms in Texas. *Educational Policy* 25 (4), 614–647.

Palmer, D.K. and Martínez, R.A. (2013) Teacher agency in bilingual spaces: A fresh look at preparing teachers to educate Latina/o bilingual children. *Review of Research in Education* 37 (1), 269–297.

Palmer, D.K. and Henderson, K.I. (2016) Dual language bilingual education placement practices: Educator discourses about emergent bilingual students in two program types. *International Multilingual Research Journal* 10 (1), 17–30.

Palmer, D.K., Martínez, R.A., Mateus, S.G. and Henderson, K. (2014) Reframing the debate on language separation: Toward a vision for translanguaging pedagogies in the dual language classroom. *The Modern Language Journal* 98 (3), 757–772.

Palmer, D.K., Henderson, K., Wall, D., Zúñiga, C.E. and Berthelsen, S. (2015) Team teaching among mixed messages: Implementing two-way dual language bilingual education at third grade in Texas. *Language Policy* 15 (4), 393–413.

Patton, M.Q. (2002) Qualitative interviewing. In M.Q. Patton (ed.) *Qualitative Research and Evaluation Methods* (pp. 344–347). Thousand Oaks, CA: Sage.

Pavlenko, A. (2002) Bilingualism and emotions. *Multilingua* 21 (1), 45–78.

Pennycook, A. (2010) *Language as a Local Practice.* London: Routledge.

Pérez, B. (2004) *Becoming Biliterate: A Study of Two-Way Bilingual Immersion Education.* Mahwah, NJ: Lawrence Erlbaum Associates.

Phillips, J.K. (2003) Implications of language education policies for language study in schools and universities. *The Modern Language Journal* 87 (4), 579–586.

Phillipson, R. and Skutnabb-Kangas, T. (1996) English only worldwide or language ecology? *TESOL Quarterly* 30 (3), 429–452.

Pimentel, C., Soto, L.D., Pimentel, O. and Urrieta, L. (2008) The dual language dualism: ¿Quiénes ganan? *TABE Journal* 10 (1), 200–223.

Potowski, K. (2004) Student Spanish use and investment in a dual immersion classroom: Implications for second language acquisition and heritage language maintenance. *The Modern Language Journal* 88 (i), 75–101.

Razfar, A. (2006) Language ideologies in practice: Repair and classroom discourse. *Linguistics and Education* 16 (4), 404–424.

Reyes, M. (2001) Unleashing possibilities: Biliteracy in the primary grades. In M. Reyes and J. Halcon (eds) *The Best for Our Children* (pp. 96–121). New York: Teachers College Press.

Reyes, S.A. and Vallone, T.L. (2007) Toward an expanded understanding of two-way bilingual immersion education: Constructing identity through a critical additive bilingual/bicultural pedagogy. *Multicultural Perspectives* 9 (3), 3–11.

Ricento, T. (2000) *Ideology, Politics and Language Policies: Focus on English* (A.D. Houwer, ed.). Philadelphia, PA: John Benjamins Publishing Company.

Ricento, T. (2005) Problems with the 'language-as-resource' discourse in the promotion of heritage languages in the USA. *Journal of Sociolinguistics* 9 (3), 348–368.

Ricento, T. (2006) Theoretical perspectives in language policy: An overview. In T. Ricento (ed.) *An Introduction to Language Policy* (pp. 3–9). Malden, MA: Blackwell.

Ricento, T. and Hornberger, N. (1996) Unpeeling the onion: Language planning and policy and the ELT professional. *TESOL Quarterly* 30 (3), 401–427.

Roediger, D.R. (2005) *Working toward Whiteness: How America's Immigrants became White: The Strange Journey from Ellis Island to the Suburbs*. New York: Basic Books.

Rolstad, K., Mahoney, K. and Glass, G.V. (2005) The big picture: A meta- analysis of program effectiveness research on English language learners. *Educational Policy* 19 (4), 572–594.

Rosa, J. (2018) *Looking Like a Language, Sounding Like a Race: Raciolinguistic Ideologies and the Learning of Latinidad*. New York: Oxford University Press.

Rosa, J. and Flores, N. (2017) Unsettling race and language: Toward a raciolinguistic perspective. *Language in Society* 46 (5), 621–647. https://doi.org/10.1017/S0047404517 000562

Roser, N., Martínez, M., Moore, H.C. and Palmer, D. (2015) Reinvite drama into classroom: Part 2, exploring stories through process drama. *IRA E-ssentials*.

Roser, N., Palmer, D., Greeter, E., Martinez, M. and Wooten, D.A. (2015) 'That isn't fair!'/'¡No es justo!' Process drama for children: Learning to think critically about picture books in English and Spanish. In D.A. Wooten and B.E. Cullinan (eds) *Children's Literature in the Reading Program: Engaging Young Readers in the 21st Century* (pp. 127–149). Newark, DE: International Literacy Association.

Ruiz, R. (1984) Orientations in language planning. *National Association for Bilingual Education Journal* 8 (2), 15–34.

Sánchez, M.T., García, O. and Solorza, C. (2017) Reframing language allocation policy in dual language bilingual education. *Bilingual Research Journal* 41 (1), 37–51.

Santa Ana, O. (2004) Chronology of events, court decisions, and legislation affecting language minority children in American public education. In O. Santa Ana (ed.) *Tongue-Tied: The Lives of Multilingual Children in Public Education* (pp. 87–106). Lanham, MD: Rowman & Littlefield.

Sayer, P. (2013) Translanguaging, TexMex, and bilingual pedagogy: Emergent bilinguals learning through the vernacular. *TESOL Quarterly* 47 (1), 63–88. https://doi. org/10.1002/tesq.53

Scanlan, M. and Palmer, D.K. (2009) Race, power, and (in)equity within two-way immersion settings. *The Urban Review* 41 (5), 391–415. https://doi.org/10.1007/s11256 -008-0111-0

Schmid, C. (2000) The politics of English only in the United States: Historical, social, and legal aspects. In R.D. González (ed.) *Language Ideologies: Critical Perspectives on the Official English Movement* (Vol. 1, pp. 64–86). Mahwah, NJ: Lawrence Erlbaum Associates.

Shohamy, E. (2006) *Language Policy: Hidden Agendas and New Approaches*. London: Routledge.

Silverman, D. and Marvasti, A. (2008) *Doing Qualitative Research: A Comprehensive Guide*. Thousand Oaks, CA: Sage.

Silverstein, M. (1979) Language structure and linguistic ideology. In P. Clyne, W. Hanks and C. Hofbauer (eds) *The Elements: A Parasession on Linguistic Units and Levels* (pp. 193–248). Chicago, IL: Chicago Linguistic Society.

Skilton-Sylvester, E. (2003) Legal discourse and decisions, teacher policymaking and the multilingual classroom: Constraining and supporting Khmer/English biliteracy in the United States. *International Journal of Bilingual Education and Bilingualism* 6 (3/4), 168–184.

Sloan, K. (2005) Playing to the logic of the Texas accountability system: How focusing on 'ratings'—not children—undermines quality and equity. In A. Valenzuela (ed.) *Leaving Children Behind: How 'Texas-Style' Accountability Fails Latino Youth* (pp. 153–178). Albany, NY: State University of New York Press.

Solano-Flores, G. and Trumbull, E. (2003) Examining language in context: The need for new research and practice paradigms in the testing of English language learners. *Educational Researcher* 32 (2), 3–13.

Steele, J.L., Slater, R.O., Zamarro, G., Miller, T., Li, J., Burkhauser, S. and Bacon, M. (2017) Effects of dual-language immersion programs on student achievement: Evidence from lottery data. *American Educational Research Journal* 54, 282S–306S.

Stritikus, T. (2003) The interrelationship of beliefs, context, and learning: The case of a teacher reacting to language policy. *Journal of Language, Identity, and Education* 2 (1), 29–52.

Stritikus, T. and Garcia, E.E. (2000) Education of limited English proficient students in California schools: An assessment of the influence of Proposition 227 on selected teachers and classrooms. *Bilingual Research Journal* 24 (1 & 2), 75–85.

Texas Education Code: Chapter 89. §89.1205. Required Bilingual Education and English as Second Language Programs. Subchapter BB. Commissioner's rules concerning state plan for educating Limited English Proficient students.

Toribio, A.J. and Bullock, B.E. (2016) A new look at heritage Spanish and its speakers. In D. Pascual y Cabo (ed.) *Advances in Spanish as a Heritage Language* (pp. 27–50). New York: John Benjamins.

Tyack, D. and Cuban, L. (1995) *Tinkering Toward Utopia: A Century of Public School Reform*. Cambridge, MA: Harvard University Press.

Umansky, I.M. and Reardon, S.F. (2014) Reclassification patterns among Latino English learner students in bilingual, dual immersion, and English immersion classrooms. *American Educational Research Journal* 51 (5), 879–912. https://doi.org/10.3102/0002831214545110

Urciuoli, B. (1995) Language and borders. *Annual Review of Anthropology* 24 (1), 525–546.

US Department of Education (2015) Our nations English learners: What are their characteristics? Data story. See https://www2.ed.gov/datastory/el -characteristics/index.html (accessed 4 December 2019).

Utah Dual Language Immersion (2018) Utah Dual Language Immersion Instructional Model. See http://www.utahdli.org/instructionalmodel.html (accessed 4 December 2019).

Valdés, G. (1997) Dual language immersion programs: A cautionary note concerning the education of language-minority students. *Harvard Educational Review* 67 (3), 391–429.

Valdés, G. (2001) *Learning and Not Learning English: Latino Students in American Schools*. New York: Teachers College Press.

Valdés, G. (2005) Bilingualism, heritage language learners, and SLA research: Opportunities lost or seized? *The Modern Language Journal* 89 (3), 410–426.

Valdés, G., Menken, K. and Castro, M. (2015) *Common Core, Bilingual and English Language Learners: A Resource for Educators*. Philadelphia, PA: Caslon Publishing.

Valdez, V.E., Delavan, G. and Freire, J.A. (2016) The marketing of dual language education policy in Utah print media. *Educational Policy* 30 (6), 849–883.

Valdiviezo, L. (2009) Bilingual intercultural education in indigenous schools: An ethnography of teacher interpretations of government policy. *International Journal of Bilingual Education and Bilingualism* 12 (1), 61–79. https://doi.org/10.1080/13670050802149515

Valenzuela, A. (1999) *Subtractive Schooling: US-Mexican Youth and the Politics of Caring*. (C. Sleeter, ed.). Albany, NY: SUNY Press.

Varghese, M.M. (2008) Using cultural models to unravel how bilingual teachers enact language policies. *Language and Education* 22 (5), 289–306.

Varghese, M.M. and Stritikus, T. (2005) 'Nadie me dijó (nobody told me)': Language policy negotiation and implications for teacher education. *Journal of Teacher Education* 56 (1), 73–87.

Weinstein, M. (2012) Text Analysis Markup System (TAMS) Analyzer. Retrieved January 19, 2020: http://tamsys.sourceforge.net/.

Wiley, T.G. and Lukes, M. (1996) English-only and standard English ideologies in the US. *TESOL Quarterly* 30 (3), 511–535.

Wilson, D.M. (2011) Dual language programs on the rise. *Harvard Education Letter* 27 (2), 1–2.

Woolard, K.A. (1998) Introduction: Language ideology as a field of inquiry. In B.B. Schieffelin, K.A. Woolard and P.V. Kroskrity (eds) *Language Ideologies: Practice and Theory* (pp. 3–47). New York: Oxford University Press.

Wright, S. (2004) *Language Policy and Planning: From Nationalism to Globalization.* New York: Palgrave Macmillan.

Zentella, A.C. (1997) *Growing Up Bilingual: Puerto Rican Children in New York.* Walden, MA: Blackwell.

Index

For Product Safety Concerns and Information please contact our EU Authorised Representative:

Easy Access System Europe

Mustamäe tee 50

10621 Tallinn

Estonia

gpsr.requests@easproject.com

www.ingramcontent.com/pod-product-compliance
Ingram Content Group UK Ltd.
Pitfield, Milton Keynes, MK11 3LW, UK
UKHW022030300626

6859IPUK00003B/33